TURBULENT TIMES
IN THE CAR INDUSTRY

Memories of a Trade Union Official at Cowley, Oxford

By

David Buckle

Front cover: Jack Jones, Ken Edwards and David Buckle at Pressed Steel Fisher in October 1969

With thanks to Grassroots Grants
for part-funding this book.

**OXFORDSHIRE
LIBRARY SERVICE**

Dedicated to

all past, present and future car workers.

Acknowledgements

I began this book in the autumn of 2010 at the suggestion of Katherine Hughes, Tutor of the 'Oxford Searchers' group, which was formed to provide support and guidance for people in the over-50s age group who want to pursue individual research projects, which often include personal memories that are recorded for future reference. I am very grateful to this group for their generous help towards the cost of printing this book.

Following a talk entitled 'The Turbulent Times at Cowley', which I recently gave to Radley History Club I was encouraged to put my experiences into writing by their chair, Christine Wootton, and by a committee member, Tony Rogerson. I am very grateful to Tony for proofreading my first draft and for his advice and his suggested changes. My thanks must go to Christine for offering to edit the book and put it into a suitable format for printing and to Stanley Baker for the final check. I am grateful also to Dian Slay for helpfully sorting out my computer problems, which occurred when I was writing the book.

I am especially indebted to my wife Beryl who carried out the first proofreading and made many helpful suggestions and corrections to the first draft. For over twenty-four years Beryl and our two sons, Alan and Peter, knew better than anyone else what life was like living with someone who was a trade union official during such turbulent and anxious times.

Hopefully no mistakes or errors will be found but if they do occur please accept my sincere apologies and I will amend the text in future editions of the book.

David Buckle   February 2011

Introduction

Why this book and why now?

It is twenty-three years since I retired as a full-time trade union official in Oxfordshire. Those years have given me time to reflect on events, which for the most part dominated my life both as a line worker at the Pressed Steel plant and as a senior union negotiator for both major plants at Cowley, plus the related companies involved with the car industry in Oxford - MG, Morris Radiators, Unipart and car delivery companies.

This book will mainly cover the two Cowley plants and span the years from 1912 to 1988 when I retired. I also intend to comment on my visit to German and Russian car plants in the 1970s and 1980s for a comparison with those in Britain.

My experiences at Cowley as a production line worker, shop steward and full-time union official involved in local, regional and national negotiations, plus other related matters will feature in this book.

I hope the reader will not mind if it is more anecdotal than analytical in content. I must leave the analysis of what went wrong at Cowley to industrial analysts. They are more skilled and less prejudiced than I am about Cowley in particular and the car industry generally.

I have noticed that academics, journalists and industrialists have all put their own point of view forward when writing about the car industry, especially with reference to Cowley. No full-time union official with experience of over 38 years has, so this book is my account and experience of important events affecting Cowley.

Throughout the period of the 1950s to 1980s, the management and most of the media have blamed the working people for the bad industrial relations in the Cowley plants. I will seek to show that a more modern and caring management could and should have prevented many of the bad conditions of work. The turbulence in the industry was due to the management's failure to invest sufficiently in plant and equipment, which allowed politically motivated people both in management and on the shop floor to have so much influence and power over hard-working employees.

Both the management who denied employees their rights and shop stewards who used their members for political purposes to suit their own ends have a considerable share of the blame for what happened in the second half of the 20th Century to the Cowley car industry. One lesson we should all learn is that political and industrial extremism, whether at the work-place or elsewhere, cannot be managed. It must be confronted and challenged by every democratic means available. That is certainly the lesson I learnt during the turbulence at the Cowley Assembly Plant.

Decent hard working people did not deserve either bad management or politically motivated extremists as shop stewards. What the employees wanted was fair pay for a fair day's work, job security, fair treatment, decent working conditions and, last but by no means least, respect and understanding of their needs.

I believe I am right in saying that British company law makes no requirement on directors and shareholders to have any obligation to be good stewards of their assets, their employees or their customers. Furthermore it is not widely recognised that institutional shareholders have a much greater power over what happens to a company than individual shareholders enjoy. It is high time both these issues were dealt with in the interests of ordinary employees, individual shareholders and customers. The constant changes in ownership of British Leyland as will be shown in Chapter 2, Part 11, were regardless of the needs or support of the employees and demonstrate the point I am making.

BMW are the present owners of the old Pressed Steel factory where they have substantially increased investment to make it the plant we should all have had from the 1950s to the 1980s. Employees now enjoy much safer working conditions in a factory, which is far cleaner, safer and much quieter than in the old days. No longer is there lead in the atmosphere causing lead poisoning, nor extremely high levels of noise causing many employees to suffer from tinnitus. Power assisted tools are banned and the factory is very clean, quiet, and much brighter compared to the appalling conditions of the past. It is also very important to employees that their unions and shop stewards are now recognised with full negotiating rights and not subjected to hostile management.

Key to abbreviations used in the book

ACAS	Advisory, Conciliation and Arbitration Service
AEU	Amalgamated Engineering Union
BAe	British Aerospace
BL	British Leyland
BLMC	British Leyland Motor Corporation
CAC	Central Arbitration Committee
GDP	Gross Domestic Product
ILO	International Labour Organisation
NNC	National Negotiating Committee
NUVB	National Union of Vehicle Builders
TGWU	Transport and General Workers Union
TUC	Trade Union Congress

Chapter 1

1930s – 1940s

The early years

The Bullnose Morris was the first car to be built by William Morris (later Lord Nuffield). By 1925 the annual output of cars was 56,000. All the car parts were brought to the Oxford Morris Motors plant by rail from the Midlands. This not only proved very expensive, it also demonstrated the need for a car body plant to be built near the new Morris Motors' assembly plant.

William Morris recruited his workers from the poor, non-unionized, Oxford service sector, i.e. low-paid shop workers, University employees and local farm workers. The Company made it clear to all new employees both blue and white-collared that unions were not welcome. Paternalism was William Morris' alternative. It is my belief that if only he had accepted the right of his employees to join a union and they had obtained negotiating rights, as the management of Pressed Steel conceded in 1936, industrial relations problems in Morris Motors from the 1960s onwards could have been very different.

Later Morris agreed to 'line representatives'. However, employees, including line representatives, who caused the management any problems, were either removed from the plant or were no longer allowed to represent their fellow workers in a way they would wish.

William Morris' Company also introduced what became known as 'The Annual Spring Clean' early in the New Year when they needed to produce more cars than during the winter months. With an increase in demand, many workers who had been laid off for several weeks were recalled. This was an opportunity for the management to tell some employees who had been 'difficult' in the past that they need not return - in effect, they were sacked.

In 1926 the new Pressed Steel plant was financed and built by the Budd Company from Philadelphia, USA, to provide the car bodies, which William Morris needed. The 'Press', as it came to be known, was an independent company and eventually produced car bodies for many car-manufacturing companies including Rover, Standard Triumph, Rolls Royce, Rootes Group and Austin Healey. For a short time, in the late 1950s, even the Ford Capri trim work on car bodies was carried out there.

Once the Pressed Steel plant had been built and recruitment begun, the Company soon discovered there was no available workforce in the Oxfordshire area. They had to implement a recruitment programme throughout the UK by advertising nationally for both skilled and semi-skilled labour. Due to the recession in the 1920s, the response came very quickly and men from the Welsh, Scottish and Yorkshire coal mines, shipyard workers from the North East and miners from the West of England china clay industry came to Oxford looking for work.

Stories were told of ex Welsh coal miners walking to Cowley to apply for jobs and dying of hunger and exhaustion on the way. Their friends buried them where they died and informed the police where the dead body was when they reached the next town. The influx of so many people meant the Cowley area enjoyed a boom in house building to accommodate them and their families.

Unlike the local people engaged by William Morris, workers not only came to live and work in the car industry from far away, but they also brought their trade union membership cards and cultures with them and quickly sought full trade union recognition and rights in the Pressed Steel.

At first the Company resisted union recognition but after several disputes and a major strike in 1936, recognition for both skilled and semi-skilled unions was obtained.

The Transport and General Workers Union (TGWU) won sole negotiating rights for all semi-skilled employees, something many firms would give their eye teeth for nowadays. In effect the Pressed Steel became a fully unionised plant by the late 1930s.

The Amalgamated Engineering Union representing toolmakers, the Electricians Union (ETU), the National Union of Vehicle Builders (NUVB), the Pattern Makers Union and some other smaller unions such as the Boilermakers, etc. followed.

The serious differences between Morris Motors and the Pressed Steel companies, in policies regarding union recognition and the rights of employees to negotiate their terms of conditions of employment through shop stewards, laid the foundation for major industrial relationship problems and the turbulent times, which began in the 1950s. In fact it was the beginning of the two plants developing totally different cultures, which survived until the late 1980s.

Chapter 2

The 1950s - Part 1

Life on the production line and factory conditions

I was demobbed from the Royal Marines in July 1946. Returning from Germany on board a merchant ship, our Company Commander told the senior officers to lecture us on how we should prepare for civilian life. I remember a Sergeant Major in particular who had vivid memories of the worst years of the depression saying he was convinced that the time had come for radical changes in the role of workers and managers. He said that in the old days the employers had all the power so they could hire and fire at will and working employees had to take whatever treatment was meted out to them. He said, "Organise yourselves into unions and get your rights through such organisations. Don't let the bastards (management) do to you what they did to us in the twenties and thirties." Bearing in mind a bad experience I had when working as a house boy for an employer in Ramsgate before I was evacuated to Radley, this advice gave me much food for thought.

On being demobbed, the Royal Marines offered me a job as a store man at HMS Hornbill, a Royal Navy air base at Culham. With no qualifications of any kind, I accepted the job they had obtained for me.

It so happened that my wife's uncle was a shop steward for the transport drivers on the base. He recruited me into the TGWU in 1947 and shortly after I had joined I was elected shop steward to represent all the other manual employees. I am now an honorary life member of the TGWU.

Some of the naval officers did not enjoy having to deal with unions, especially shop stewards, and certainly not an ex Royal Marine Sergeant. Whenever I failed to reach an agreement I called in the Local District Officer much to their anger. They didn't like matters being taken out of the base and found full-time officials even more difficult to deal with than me.

By 1950 and with two sons to bring up, my wife and I found it difficult to manage on £5.7s.6d per week so I decided to apply for a job at the Pressed Steel where I knew earnings were much higher. I was offered a job as a line worker, which I accepted not realising what I was letting myself into. I had no idea what a profound difference it would make to my life, my wife and family in so many ways, which the remainder of this book will show.

After an interview with the Personnel Manager, Jim Howse, I was taken on to the shop floor to see which job they required me to do.

My first shock was the condition of the factory. It was filthy, very dark and extremely noisy, with lead dust in the atmosphere, which glittered when the sun shone through the very high, filthy windows. Due to smoke from gas and arc welding guns it was very difficult to see much beyond fifty yards. All the men looked very pale. To me it was Dante's inferno. I nearly changed my mind about working there.

The job I was offered was to operate a spot welding gun, which I noticed sent sparks flying everywhere. I accepted the job I was shown and was told to report for work on the following Monday. I was also told I would be on 'piecework' and my pay would be about £15 a week depending on how much work the gang completed. (When someone is hired to do piecework they are paid on how much they produce rather than a flat hourly rate). The working week then was forty-two hours and was subject to occasional overtime depending on the demand for cars.

We had to be ready to start work when the works' hooter sounded and the line started to move. I expected to do the job I had accepted on my first visit to the plant. To my surprise I was told to do a totally different job, i.e. working on a punching jig making several holes into a car side panel. I told the foreman I had not accepted that job and wished to be put on the one I had accepted. When he refused and told me in no uncertain terms to do as I was told, I asked for the shop steward.

Having been informed by the foreman and me what the problem was, the shop steward said to me, "Do the job you have been given."

After I protested about the problem and asked for his support he turned to the foreman and shouted, "We are going to have trouble with this one", which left me with no alternative but to accept what had happened. Given my involvement in the car industry for the next forty years, neither the foreman, the shop steward nor I realised at the time how prophetic the shop steward's words to the foreman turned out to be.

I soon discovered how large the plant was. I was told it was even larger than Hyde Park. The production facilities consisted of several production lines, sub areas for producing car doors and chassis, etc., three huge press shops stamping out car parts, three paint shops and two trim shops, plus a very large tool room and die park. There was a very small employee car park because only a few workers could afford cars in those days. At the beginning and end of each shift, Garsington Road close to the two factories was a 'river' of bicycles with no room for cars.

The factory had its own hospital (very much used due to the amount of accidents), a dental clinic, fire station, railway system and, finally, a huge office block and the head office.

There were seven different canteens. Two were for manual workers with plain tables and bench seats while foremen had a slightly better canteen with salt and pepper pots. Supervisors had knives and forks, plus a jug of water and glasses. White-collar workers had their own canteen. Area managers had a properly laid table, as did more senior managers. Finally the directors had their own private dining room with waiters. There was one much smaller dining room called the Japanese Room with very expensive wallpaper, which was used for special guests and it had a butler who served the meals. Every employee knew which canteen they could use and would never dare to go in any other.

Once, when three of us tried to order food in the foremen's canteen because of a wider choice of menu, we were ordered out. As far as eating in canteens was concerned, the class system was well and truly established.

Line gangs consisted of anything up to eighty people and all money earned was shared. If older men couldn't keep up, the gang demanded that they were removed. This often brought me into conflict with other members of the gang as I sought to protect older people from being discriminated against because of their age. In such circumstances, the piecework system often set worker against worker.

Sparks from welding guns burnt our clothes and woe betide anyone who failed to wear safety glasses because it was very easy to lose an eye. Special industrial gloves had to be worn to prevent serious cuts from sharp metal.

If we needed to go to the toilet we did what was called 'work the line,' which meant we had to signal to the foreman that we wished to go to the toilet. When permission was given, we then had to work as far back as possible down the line then run like hell to the toilet, run back, and hope the next car body had not gone too far from your normal working space. If it had, we were in trouble with our fellow line workers.

About this time I was elected as a shop steward. In this capacity I sometimes needed to go to another building to see either the area supervisor or the senior shop steward about bad working conditions. Men often complained about my absence as one man missing from the gang could affect production levels and earnings.

A good example of this was one hot summer when we were complaining about excessive heat and wanted the windows in the roof to be removed. I was away from the gang for about an hour talking to the area supervisor to see what could be done to make our conditions better. When I returned, members of the gang wanted to know what I had managed to achieve. When I told them the windows would be removed, several men complained saying that I should have demanded an extra ten shillings a day for the bad conditions and not talk about removing windows. Sadly this was one of the side effects of the piecework system when people put earnings above better working conditions.

Very often the windows were removed to cool the plant down. If a summer storm arrived, rain poured down on to the electrical equipment, which gave us a nice firework display. However, it meant that we were sent home until the mess and flooded floor could be cleaned up. It was a good example of the lack of investment in air conditioning in the plant.

'Piecework' was very boring. The vast majority of workers repeated the same task, on average, every two minutes. If two people were working together, it was difficult to speak to each other, due to the noise. We dreaded being moved from one line to another because it meant we had to use different muscles, which proved very painful.

TGWU shop stewards weekend school. Iffley, Oxford 1950
Top row from the right - 6th John Green, 11th Frank Pickstock.
Bottom row from left, 1st Maxi Parker, 4th Jack Thomas (Oxon Ass. Sec.
of TGWU), 5th Harry Nicolas (Ass. Gen. Sec. TGWU),
9th Josh Murphy (Sen. Shop Steward, Pressed Steel).

It was the task of shop stewards to negotiate the piecework rate when new models were introduced. Operators learned to maximise their time to do the task being timed by the rate-setter and then to reduce it substantially after a rate had been agreed.

This was always a difficult time for shop stewards because it involved them in a battle not only with the rate-setter, but also with the management and very often their own members. Once a rate had been set, it could not be changed by either side. This was one of the reasons why the employers complained that they had lost control of the wages systems during the 1970s.

They did not like being reminded that it was they who had introduced the piecework system in the first place, to encourage higher productivity.

Because the factory was so dark and miserable, many workers placed coloured paper on their jigs to relieve their eyes. Everyone living in Cowley knew who the car workers were because of their pale complexions. The only time we had a sunburnt face was after the summer holidays.

However, there was one advantage about 'piecework'. Because we had no need to think about what we were doing, our minds wandered in all sorts of directions. Some of us solved the problem of boredom by redesigning our gardens and homes whilst working. This may be the reason why DIY, etc. was so successful and DIY companies always made sure their shops were close to the factories. This was the more creative parts of workers' lives. I was never any good at DIY so I started visiting art galleries, museums and listening to classical music to help take my mind off the appalling job I had, which gave me, like others, no job satisfaction.

I was once working in tandem with another man where if anything went wrong we would know immediately. One morning after the tea break at 9.00 a.m. we restarted, following each other round the jig. I began to think about a speech I intended to make at the Banbury Town Hall that evening at a Labour Party meeting. Suddenly my mate signalled, "That's it Dave, time for lunch." I couldn't remember what I had done between 9.15 a.m. and 12.45 p.m. Nothing could have gone wrong because it would have broken my train of thought. I then realised how vulnerable workers were to accidents in such situations.

When I arrived at Banbury Town Hall that evening, the chairman asked me where my speech notes were. I replied, "In my head."

Short-time working and massive redundancies were never far from our minds as job security was not on offer by the management. That came through negotiations many years later. In the 1950s and 60s hire purchase tax was a major cause of either short-time working or demands to work overtime for two hours from 5.15 - 7.15 p.m. Cycling home after such a long hard day was no fun, bearing in mind I had left Radley at 6.30 am and cycled six miles to the factory.

If we were shut out due to low demand for cars we were guaranteed £12 per week. Very often the management tried various methods to avoid making this payment - two in particular:

1. They would instruct line inspectors to 'chalk up' the slightest fault, which delayed the lines. (If they wanted more production they would tell the inspectors to 'put your chalk away').

2. The management often broke an agreement in the expectation that workers would go on strike. Having left the factory the workers would be informed not to return until required. On returning, they would be told they were not entitled to guaranteed pay because they had been on strike.

Some stewards had very good relations with their foremen who warned them when they had to shut people out for a few days or even weeks and had been instructed to break an agreement. In those circumstances, shop stewards made sure there was no strike and dealt with the problem on their return to work, thus ensuring everyone received their guaranteed pay.

Due to much short-time working and redundancies, workers began to challenge management on their production figures. This meant they started to read and understand the national figures about sales and storage of completed cars and challenged the Company on the need for higher production levels if necessary.

It would not be too far fetched to say this was the beginning of employee participation and their more detailed enquiries into management control and power over job security.

I worked in the Pressed Steel for fourteen years as a line worker and was an active shop steward for nine. In that time I learned a great deal about trade unionism through their courses and what we could, or could not, achieve by collective bargaining. One important lesson I learned, which I later taught new shop stewards, was not to preach socialism to the management. The only thing they wanted to hear was what we, as stewards, wanted from them and how much it would cost.

The 1950s – Part 2

Union demands for recognition

at Morris Motors

In 1952, the Austin-Morris Company merged with the British Motor Corporation (BMC).

In 1953, BMC took over the Fisher and Ludlow Company. Many takeovers occurred in later years and became a major problem for all employees with all the uncertainties of holding their jobs and avoiding redundancies.

Three unions, the AEU, TGWU and the ETU, began demanding the right for full union recognition in Morris Motors, which the management resisted, maintaining the opposition William Morris had always demanded towards trade unionism and anyone who wished to challenge their managerial role.

The struggle for the Company to recognise shop stewards was a denial of employees' rights, causing major problems in industrial relations for the future. If only William Morris had followed the example of the Pressed Steel management his plant may well have escaped serious problems later on. Instead, he laid the foundations for what was to follow - bad industrial relations and extremist shop stewards, with political rather than industrial relations objectives, getting elected. Such people forgot their role was to represent all members, regardless of their political views.

Eventually partial recognition was agreed in 1956 after a major strike when some employees from the Pressed Steel who were producing car bodies for Morris Motors also went on strike in solidarity with their fellow workers. Having won partial recognition, Morris Motors' employees and shop stewards soon found out that trade union recognition did not amount to much.

The Company still insisted on recognising line representatives and were not happy having also to deal with union shop stewards whom they made sure were failing to achieve very much for their members. I saw some of this when I was sent to work in Morris Motors doing final repairs on car bodies before handing them over to Morris Motors. One day I recruited seventeen employees into the TGWU. When the management found out what I had done they told the Pressed Steel to take me back as I was no longer acceptable to them.

Having obtained jobs in Morris Motors, a small group of Trotskyites laid low for a time. When the opportunity came for the election of shop stewards, they put their names forward claiming they could, and would, achieve far more than line representatives and the few shop stewards had managed to do.

Most of the very militant stewards made sure members had no idea about their real motives.

Having been elected for two years their tactic was to persuade a small group of members to stop work until their demands were met. Anyone who carried on working discovered later that the stewards had informed management the work done during the dispute was 'black' and could not be worked on when the dispute ended. This in turn had a much wider effect on many others elsewhere in the plant.

With the car industry booming in the immediate post war years and the German, Japanese, French and Italian industries struggling to re-build their car industries, demand for British cars was very high, so the Company were terrified of any stoppage due to strikes, etc. This was the opportunity for extreme left-wing members in Morris Motors to be even more effective in their demands. Because the management often conceded without any thought for the consequences, militant trade unionism was demonstrating that this was the way to beat their employees.

As a result, Morris Motors throughout the 1960s, 70s and 80s was beset with industrial disputes, which became part of the plant's culture and it became known nationally as a strike-prone plant with unions getting most of the blame.

Constant stoppages of small sections had a much wider effect on the rest of the production line, meaning that hundreds of other workers could no longer work and were shut out without pay, including the Pressed Steel who were supplying the car bodies.

Industrial relations reporters from the media in general were forever coming to Cowley, standing on the picket lines and interviewing anyone whom they could find. Later, as a full-time official, I was in constant demand by the press, radio and TV to make statements about the growing crisis.

Eventually the situation became so serious that a Commission of Enquiry was set up by the Society of Motor Manufacturers and Trades, jointly chaired by Bill Carron, President of the AEU, and Leslie Blakeman, Personnel Director of Fords, to enquire into poor industrial relations and industrial trouble at the assembly plant.

Despite the fact I was not at that time the TGWU officer responsible for the plant, I was told by Jack Jones to represent our union at the enquiry.

After lengthy submissions by both management and the three unions, TGWU, AEU and the ETU, on the first day, Bill Carron, on behalf of the management side, invited the union side to join them for lunch. Malcolm Young the AEU Oxford District Secretary replied, "Brother Carron, I never accept management's invitations to eat with them", and left to go elsewhere.

On our way to the restaurant I heard Blakeman say to Carron, "What's the matter with your District Secretary?"

Carron replied, "The Belfast bastard!" It was then that I remembered that Carron was a Catholic, and Young was a Protestant.

Very little was agreed or came out of the enquiry and the disputes continued at an even greater pace. Neither management at Morris Motors nor the militant stewards seemed to have any idea how to talk and agree with one another.

Extreme militancy never established a foothold in the Pressed Steel and was never likely to. A well-organised shop steward structure saw to that. Most of the credit for good industrial relations was due to Jack Thomas, the Oxford District Secretary of the TGWU, and Josh Murphy, the Senior Shop Steward, plus other branch officers and members.

It is important to point out that if a group of members felt the need for a dispute, they had to put their case to all the TGWU stewards (175 plus). If the latter agreed, the workers in dispute as well as the management would know they had the full support of every member. If not, they were on their own. This was the reason why the Pressed Steel hardly ever had a strike among production workers.

Such matters were dealt with very differently in Morris Motors where individual members of both unions, whilst not agreeing with the militant shop stewards' political aims - if they even knew them - went along with them by holding sectional strikes because they thought they would gain financially.

In effect, the extremist union stewards were trying to run a union within a union and eventually became a greater danger to their members' job prospects than the inefficient poor management.

In this chapter I have tried to explain what I believe were the basic reasons for different industrial relations problems and their cause in Morris Motors compared to the Pressed Steel.

Chapter 3

The 1960s

A decade of merger mania and its consequences

In May 1963 Jack Thomas, the much respected Oxfordshire District Secretary informed me that he would be retiring at the end of the year and hoped that I would apply for his position. After discussing this with my wife, I decided to apply when the opportunity came.

In the autumn of 1963 I was invited, along with ten other applicants, for an interview at the TGWU's regional offices in Birmingham. We were to be interviewed by Jack Jones, then the Midland Regional Secretary.

Following a very testing interview just before Christmas, a letter arrived from Frank Cousins, our union's General Secretary, informing me I had been appointed to be the Oxfordshire District Secretary and to report for work at the Oxford office on January 4th 1964. My pay was to be the princely sum of £20 per week. At that time I was earning on average £36 a week in the factory.

I had not only accepted a job with a substantial cut in earnings, I had also doubled my hours of work from an average of forty hours to over seventy hours per week. However, there was one huge advantage; I now had job satisfaction and was no longer working for capitalism. I didn't realise it at the time, but it turned out to be one of the most significant events in my life.

I reported to the Cowley Road district office on 4th January 1964 and was received with a very kind welcome by Jack

Thomas and his secretary, June Mott. June was a first-class secretary and stayed with me as my secretary until I retired in 1988. The other officer was Cliff Crawley, the man whom I had to deal with when I was employed at Culham, who also gave me a very warm welcome. To me it was a good start with colleagues I knew I could work with.

My first shock was to discover the range of firms and industries I would be involved in when I took over from Jack in August 1964.

First day as District Secretary, taking over from Jack Thomas. January 4th 1964. Photograph courtesy of the *Oxford Mail and Times.*

I needed the six months with Jack Thomas because he took me round to each firm to learn the many different agreements, 'custom and practices' they were engaged in. The workers included not only those at the Pressed Steel, (the Assembly Plant was the responsibility of Cliff Crawley), but also road haulage drivers, blanket workers at Witney, cement workers at Shipton-on-Cherwell, local authority manual workers and county roadmen based in Witney. I was also responsible for Government industrial workers at the Central Ordnance Depot, Bicester, white-collar employees at the Pressed Steel and Smiths Industries HGV drivers at Witney. I became responsible for nearly 10,000 members and soon discovered I was on a steep learning curve.

Just before Jack Thomas retired I asked him how our office came to be in the Cowley Road. His reply surprised me. He told me that Ernie Bevin, our union's General Secretary said he wanted to visit Oxford and talk about organising new members, other than car workers, in industries in Oxford. They met in Jack's home, near the factories. At one point Bevin asked Jack where his office was. Jack replied, "Here in my home".

Bevin replied, "We must do something about that, let's go for a walk down the Cowley Road and see what we can find."

They set off down the Cowley Road. On arriving at the major bus station Jack said, "This may be a place to look."

Bevin said, "No, it's too near the car factories. We are a general workers' union, Jack, and we should demonstrate to future members in other industries we are not in Oxfordshire just for car workers and bus drivers."

They continued until they got to The Plain where Ernie suggested they return back up the Cowley Road to number 46 Cowley Road, then a small bookshop. Bevin walked in and asked the owner if he would like to sell it. He replied, "Yes, providing the price is right." Bevin offered him £340, which was immediately accepted.

I think that story illustrates the wisdom and vision of Bevin because he knew we would have to recruit members from a wide range of industries in Oxfordshire and must not be seen to be interested only in car workers.

Merger mania

- 1961 Jaguar took over Daimler and Leyland took over Standard Triumph.

- 1966 Pressed Steel merged with Fisher and Ludlow and became Pressed Steel Fisher, part of BMC. BMC and Jaguar merged as British Motor Holdings (BMH) and Leyland took over Rover Group.

- 1967. Chrysler took over the Rootes Group.

- 1968 Leyland and BMC merged to form BLMC. The Pressed Steel also merged to become part of BLMC.

A deal that the Pressed Steel should become part of BMH was completed at Chequers late one evening after dinner between the Prime Minister, Harold Wilson, George Harriman of BMH and Donald Stokes from Leyland.

I commented later that bearing in mind these three men spent the evening together, it's not surprising such a bastard had been created. I made that comment because I thought it would never succeed after Stokes said he knew nothing about how cars were produced. It's interesting to note that Michael Edwardes made similar remarks when he became boss of BLMC, on the insistence of the Prime Minister, Mrs Thatcher, in 1977. Neither comment inspired workers to have any confidence in the top man.

I am a big fan of E F Schumacher, who wrote a book in 1973 entitled *Small is beautiful*. It is my belief the creation of British Leyland and it's eventual downfall, proves his point.

Back to the causes of Cowley turbulence

Between 1952 and 1988 there were eleven mergers and changes of name, all of which in one form or another affected both Cowley factories and the morale of their employees. Many of the mergers meant the end of local bargaining agreements and many workers' rights. It also brought large-scale redundancies and short-time working with the consequent loss of jobs and earnings.

One example was the Rootes Group being taken over by Chrysler. This merger caused serious problems for the Pressed Steel plant as 47% of all car bodies were produced there for the Rootes Group. When Chrysler announced they would be taking their custom elsewhere, real panic set in with both management and workers.

At the request of the Pressed Steel management and our members, I went to the Rootes Group factory in Coventry to plead with the directors not to withdraw their business. Their reply was short and sharp, "We are not going to give our work and future plans for new models to a company who is our major competitor and that includes the Pressed Steel who are now part of' BLMC."

The withdrawal from Cowley of car body production for its major customer at Ryton also caused substantial redundancies. Future models were not on the planning board at that time, which was an additional problem for the Pressed Steel and its employees.

In view of these mergers, it is now necessary for me to refer to the Pressed Steel factory as the Body Plant and Morris Motors as the Assembly Plant.

Bargaining locally was challenged by the management following the mergers. This in turn also meant that local agreements no longer mattered to them as they wanted to end all of them and have company-wide bargaining instead, which covered more than one plant throughout the UK.

One of their reasons they explained to me was that BMH were very keen to control wage bargaining - in particular the piecework system. Skilled employees were also targeted about their wages and their 'custom and practices', which management believed was out of date.

In all fairness both the piecework system and skilled rates of pay needed being brought up-to-date. It was how this was to be achieved and whether a negotiated agreement was possible, which caused much anguish and set my mind racing as to how this could be obtained without further major disputes.

Towards the end of the sixties the Company informed me that they wanted to introduce a new grade structure for all skilled and semi-skilled employees. This raised some very serious problems for the four skilled unions and the TGWU representing semi-skilled employees in the Body Plant. We had always thought the Company placed a higher value on their skilled employees than our members, as they were more difficult to recruit than semi-skilled people.

This was proved to be the case several years later when I calculated there had been a real reduction in wages for semi-skilled employees compared to skilled men. I discovered that production workers' pay had declined by 73% compared with that of skilled employees who had suffered a 34% decline between 1971 and 1981.

Whilst skilled men had virtual job security and no short-time working, our members, especially production workers, suffered from often being shut out of work with the resulting reduction in earnings. We argued also that, whilst skilled men could spend their whole working lives earning regular wages each week, production workers not only lost earnings through short-time working but could not keep up with their work so easily after they were fifty-plus and therefore took a substantial reduction in income.

Following major discussions over several months between unions and then with management over a new pay structure in the Body Plant, no agreement could be reached and the issue went to a 'final stage conference'. In attendance were national trade union leaders, district officials and senior shop stewards.

At one point during the conference when things were a bit heated, John Boyd, General Secretary of the Amalgamated Engineering Union, (AEU), an active Salvation Army man said, "Brothers, before we vote, can I suggest we have five minutes of quiet contemplation and pray to God for guidance and advice."

The TGWU Senior Steward, Josh Murphy, replied, "And which union does He belong to?" Votes were important in that situation!!!

As no agreement could be reached, either between unions or with the Company, through the 'disputes procedures', all the parties agreed that the issue should go to the Department of

Employment in London to see if their officials could assist. After extensive discussions and negotiations, with the aid of senior conciliation officers from the Department, an agreement was finally reached by the Company and each union to introduce a new pay structure.

During the day, fire engines were called to the building. In the national press the following day they reported that militants from the Cowley car industry had tried to set light to the Department. This was typical of the media as we all learnt over the years.

Disputes continued unabated at the Assembly Plant. It has to be admitted that the militants were always much better organised than our union in their leafleting tactics to members and in beating management in negotiations.

The so-called Noose Trial at Cowley Assembly Plant, 1966

I had an early and unexpected introduction to the problems of militancy in the Assembly Plant in April 1966. Normally I was not responsible for our members there, it being covered by my other colleague, Cliff Crawley our District Organiser, but he was away on holiday.

A General Election had been called the previous month. During March a serious dispute over bonus pay had arisen, followed by one-day strikes over the issue. The senior shop stewards alleged that eight members ignored the strike and tried to work and had been asked to attend a mass meeting and explain themselves and give an undertaking they would honour strike decisions in the future. They were also asked to give their earnings to a charity of their choosing, which they agreed to do.

The mass meeting had been held on the Company's premises and the so-called strike breakers were present. When they arrived at the meeting they were asked to stand under a gantry during the meeting. Someone threw a rope over the gantry to make it look like a noose. Later, one of the strike breakers mentioned it to a press reporter from the *Daily Mirror*. The next day, the *Daily Mirror* headline was, 'Workers tried under a hanging noose'. As it was the first week of a General Election it came like manna from heaven for the Conservative Party. They did their best to put the blame on the Prime Minister, Harold Wilson. A few days later the Lord Chancellor, Quinton Hogg wrote in the Daily Express:

> I find it impossible to believe that this really happened in Oxford, which I have known and loved all my life. Responsibility rests squarely with the Prime Minister, as leader of the Labour Party. His party is financed and controlled by the unions.

I noticed he omitted to say his own party has always been bankrolled largely by major industrialists and their companies!

Our General Secretary, Jack Jones, instructed me to bring the dispute to a rapid end as he believed it would do the Labour Party no good in the eyes of the electorate, given the amount of national coverage the press was giving to the issue.

I informed the branch officers that a special branch meeting should be called, at which I intended to be present and I would propose a motion to the meeting, which the General Secretary had suggested, to call the dispute off with the promise of seeking negotiations to resolve matters. About three hundred members were present. I proposed that the one-day strikes be called off with a promise that I would seek an early meeting with the Company to try and negotiate a settlement of the original dispute over bonus payments. I was met with considerable hostility. It was proposed, and seconded that the General Secretary and Buckle 'go and f*** themselves'.

I persisted in addressing the meeting, reminding members of the huge media team of press, radio and TV waiting outside for the result. I stood my ground saying it was important for the wider trade union movement that we should not give the Tories vital ammunition to attack the Labour Movement and us. After two very difficult hours of fierce argument and discussion, the motion proposed by the militants, much to their anger and my surprise, was defeated and my alternative proposal was accepted.

On leaving the meeting, held at the Cowley Workers' Club, I was confronted by a horde of press, radio and TV reporters. It was an experience I had never had and one I had to get used to in the future.

Later I got into 'hot water' with the militant stewards for saying our union was faced with 'anarchy within the plant', a comment which received national headlines in the media. The militants called on the union to conduct an inquiry into my conduct but the union took no action against me. An inquiry was held conducted by Harry Urwin, at that time our Assistant Regional Secretary, regarding the so-called 'Noose Trial'. It also covered the reasons for the dispute and the press reports about the 'Noose Trial'. I assisted the three-day inquiry by collecting evidence.

A few days later Urwin produced his report and findings and informed me he would be clearing the branch officers from any blame, claiming the whole issue had been dreamed up by the press at the beginning of a General Election to harm Labour. I strongly advised him not to take that line but, if he insisted, he should inform the Senior Shop Steward, Bob Fryer, and get his reaction first. Fryer knew what I knew and did not want to be proved a liar by me. When Urwin told Fryer of his intention Bob reacted with horror because he knew it could not all be blamed on the media. Urwin's final report, on Bob's request, was to make a general statement outlining the problems when workers were faced with serious differences of opinion between themselves, their unions and a hard-line management, on how a pay dispute should be pursued and resolved. Harry Urwin also absolved me of any blame for my comments about 'anarchy in the plant'.

As a result of this dispute, I realised how lucky I was to be responsible for our membership in the Pressed Steel where shop stewards and branch officers did not behave in the way militant branch officers and shop stewards did in Morris Motors. The 'Noose Trial' issue also taught me how to deal with a major industrial dispute and the national media. What I learned very quickly was that the media are much more interested in a good story and never let the facts get in their way.

Chapter 4

The 1970s – Part 1

Agreement on 'Mutuality' reached at the Body Plant

In 1970, the Company informed me that a new car model, the Marina, due to be built at the Body Plant would not be on the piecework system of pay and threatened that if there was opposition to this then the car would not be built at Cowley. I thought this was none other than industrial blackmail so had to decide whether to call their bluff or not.

In view of the fact that the Body Plant had had an 18-month period of short-time working, due in large part to the Rootes Group withdrawal, our members felt that we were in no position to fight and we should get the best deal possible.

We knew the management wanted to introduce a system called 'measured day work'. This is a system whereby the Company decides by the use of industrial engineers, a control mechanism based on engineered time standards, which determines how many employees will be required to do a certain job, what speed they work at and what their hourly rate of pay will be. In effect, total management control. There would be no real role for shop stewards in such a system compared to piecework. My suggestion for an 'incentive pay system' instead of measured day work was rejected by the Company who were not even prepared to consider one.

I warned management that measured day work would mean a reduction in productivity because employees would not work as fast and as hard as on 'piecework'. In fact I was eventually proved right because after 'Mutuality' had been agreed and introduced, the manpower on the production lines increased by about 27%. I chided management that this was their solution to unemployment. Manning levels became a big problem for the Company when plant managers complained that the problems of piecework had been switched to those of manning levels.

Having worked on piecework for fourteen years, I knew its good points and bad points. Its good points were that shop stewards had a role to play in determining what the rate of pay would be. We also knew what we had to do each day and once the schedule had been completed, we could go home.

The bad points were that we were subject to varying earnings according to high or low schedules - thus there was no guaranteed pay or real job security. Another problem was that, if a gang wanted to increase their earnings they either had some members removed from the gang or, worse still, insisted that older men be removed from the section because they could not keep up with younger men, which affected earnings for the rest of the gang. Some of my most difficult meetings with our members occurred when they argued that I should insist on the removal of older men, which went against my better judgement.

Before any negotiations could take place on a change of pay systems I advised the Company I had three major concerns:

1.   Were management determined to introduce measured day work or were they willing to listen to any alternatives we may wish to make? They replied that they wanted measured day work and no other system.

2.   What were their actual terms for moving from piecework to any other form of payment? They replied, "That would depend on what deal was eventually agreed."

3.   Were the Company going to try to obtain a piecework effort for a fixed hourly rate? They replied, "No."

I informed the Company I needed to talk to our Senior Shop Steward, Bill Roche, and the branch officers to be followed by a meeting of all the shop stewards to obtain their agreement, or otherwise, to start negotiations.

Following these meetings where I explained what had been going on, it was agreed that we should start the negotiations and report back on any progress made but under no circumstances agree anything until stewards and members knew the whole package and it would be they who would make the final decision.

I then began to form my ideas as to what I thought we should negotiate for in respect of maintaining, as far as possible, that line workers had as much control over their work as the piecework system provided. Measured day work would not do that but maybe some sort of employee participation might.

I had long believed in worker participation as an alternative to management dictates. As a Governor of Ruskin College, I had had several discussions with John Hughes, then the Deputy Principal of the College, on the subject and learned a lot from him about the best approach. His advice was of enormous value to me in such important negotiations.

Having discussed the matter with Bill Roche we devised a system in December 1970 called 'Mutuality'. This provided that if the Company wanted to increase line speeds, add or remove workers from the line, or change methods of working, mutual agreement must be reached jointly between shop stewards, members and management before any changes were made.

As this system reflected the kind of controls we had a right to under piecework and as it had the full support of our senior steward, branch officers and shop stewards, I felt confident to go to the next stage and inform the management accordingly. I suspected they would not agree to concede their 'right to manage' and would resist what we wanted to achieve.

I therefore requested a meeting with our newly elected General Secretary, Jack Jones, who invited me to meet him in London with Moss Evans, our union's National Secretary for the Automotive Industry. I outlined in detail what I meant by 'Mutuality' to them. After a short meeting Jack and Moss both agreed with what we were planning to do. Jack said, "If you run into any difficulties, tell management you have my full support." With his confidence and support I returned to Oxford.

This proved a wise move. Initially the management were horrified at our suggestions for clawing back some control for the workers over their conditions. At one stage in the negotiations when things became difficult, I told them we had the full support of our General Secretary. They changed their proposals, which avoided a breakdown and made it possible for the real negotiations to begin. In January 1971 both sides met to begin the task of reaching an agreement.

We met for sixty-six hours over that month. Our team consisted of Bill Roche, Tony Williamson (Branch Chairman), Alec Morton (Branch Secretary), and myself. The discussions were some of the most difficult I have ever been involved in. At one point I needed to invoke Jack's promise of his support and that removed the final obstacle to a 'Mutuality Agreement' - the first of its kind in the British and European car industries. The agreement included an ex-gratia payment of £40 to each line worker, as compensation for giving up the piecework system.

Having agreed in principal subject to the agreement also of shop stewards and members, our next stage was to take the 'Mutuality Agreement' to a special shop stewards' meeting and seek their approval, which after a lengthy meeting was given. We asked the stewards to take the document to their members, explain it and report back their views to Bill Roche. Shop stewards reported that the response was very good. We then decided to hold a mass meeting of 5,000 members where Bill Roche and I explained what the 'Mutuality Agreement' really meant.

Despite a few members voting against, the vast majority voted in favour, which gave us permission to finalise negotiations. The Agreement was eventually signed by Bill Roche, Tony Williamson and myself on the 10th February 1971.

The signing of the Mutuality Agreement at Pressed Steel Fisher, Cowley, by David Buckle (TGWU) and Ken Bradbury (PSF). February 1971

It provided in addition to 'Mutuality' a forty-hour week and a weekly wage of £42, a full shift guarantee, lay off pay, increased holiday pay and several other improvements on pay and conditions.

Moss Evans commented later, "Management didn't have a chance bearing in mind they were dealing with three magistrates and a worker/priest", meaning me, Bill and Alec who were magistrates and Tony the worker/priest.

All our shop stewards were advised that in future saying 'no' was not an option for either management or them. What it did mean was that both sides should work hard to reach a mutual agreement on line speeds, movement of labour and effort. The agreement stood the test of time for both sides and lasted for nine years without a dispute until Michael Edwardes arrived and unilaterally abandoned it. Disputes about line speeds and effort, etc. soon returned as we predicted.

Six weeks after the Body Plant agreement had been reached and implemented, the management in the Assembly Plant intended to introduce it there. The deal was accepted by a mass meeting but the senior steward and other militant stewards who were opposed to it reported back to the Company claiming it had been defeated.

Senior managers told me later that when stewards came to their office and claimed the vote had been against the scheme, they replied, "Well in that case why are they all returning to work?" Despite 'Mutuality' being introduced in the Assembly Plant, against the wishes of senior and deputy senior stewards, it made no difference to sectional strike rates, which if anything increased. The strikes were about minor matters - but not against 'Mutuality'.

The 1970s – Part 2
The Ryder Report and its consequences

In 1971 the *Sunday Times* published an article,

'How British Leyland failed the three-year test'. It read:

> The collapse of BL's profits from £40m to £3.9m marks the most important management failure in British industry over the last three years.

> No efforts to blame unions, or the Government, or the legacy of the distant past can conceal this fact.

> The history of the merger between Leyland and British Motor Holdings announced three years ago has been one long tale of mistakes made by managers who rushed into thinking they knew all the answers, and only slowly began to realise the complexity of the appalling problems, which confronted them.

Ryder, in his report also revealed that BL between 1968 and 1974 had net profits of £74m. The Company retained £4m for investment and gave shareholders £70m by way of dividend.

Twenty-one years later, in 1992, a book, *The Breakdown of Austin Rover* written by Karel Williams, John Williams and Colin Haslam, concluded:

> The failure of the business strategy by Austin Rover can clearly be attributed to faulty management decisions, the organisation of production and above all marketing.

In 1974 Tony Benn, then the Secretary of State for Trade and Industry, announced in Parliament he was seeking authority for a £50 million guarantee to British Leyland. Meanwhile, a Team of Inquiry headed by Sir Don Ryder would advise on

Leyland's situation. The Ryder Report was presented to Parliament in April 1975 and among its recommendations were policies which would have a profound effect on collective bargaining and unions in the future. Under the heading 'Industrial Democracy' was the following:

> Workers' representatives need to be given more information about their company so that they can better appreciate management's problems and co-operate more constructively in solving those problems.

The other important recommendations affecting the unions came under the heading – 'Collective Bargaining'. It stated that there should be a substantial reduction in the number of bargaining units in BL and that there should be one bargaining unit for hourly-rated employees and another for white-collar employees.

The first recommendation about industrial democracy presented no real problems for trade unions, especially in Oxford as we had campaigned for many years for the right to be kept informed by management of matters affecting our members' job prospects, etc. The recommendations about industrial democracy suited us fine. It was exactly what we wanted, as I mentioned in Chapter 2 Part 2.

The recommendation regarding collective bargaining reforms presented a much greater problem for all unions, particularly ours, as there were 58 different agreements throughout BL with different grades and rates of pay.

For many years, the craft unions had objected to the line workers' earnings being higher than theirs. However, they conveniently forgot that production workers had no real job security and earnings could fluctuate considerably from one week to another. In addition, when an operator was unable through age, etc. to keep up with the speed of the line, they had to take a much lower paid job so their earnings were reduced considerably. Skilled men however maintained their level of earnings until they retired whatever their age and fitness and enjoyed job security, a luxury we were denied.

The suggestion to move from fifty-eight bargaining units to one gave the craft unions the opportunity to correct what they thought were anomalies on pay so they began a campaign for parity across the Company. This suited management who also wanted parity. The AEU Senior Steward representing toolmakers in the Body Plant began a campaign for parity. When the Company refused, not wanting to have a local plant agreement, toolmakers went on a four-week strike, which nearly bankrupted BL. The strike ended with a failure for the AEU.

I don't enjoy saying this but a recommendation for national bargaining also played into the hands of the national unions' officials, as it would give them the considerably greater role they had not had before. They never liked plant bargaining because the power to bargain on pay for all employees lay with senior stewards and local full-time officials. National officials would only ever get involved if local officials asked for them or if a matter were referred to the 'disputes procedure' at national level by either the management or unions.

This situation was made worse for the TGWU by the fact that our National Official, Grenville Hawley, was an ex-NUVB official. He became the TGWU's National Secretary for the automotive industry after the merger of the NUVB with the TGWU in 1972. It was well known that he had objected to the merger, which had been agreed in a ballot of NUVB members, and he was therefore a reluctant member of the TGWU.

Hawley being a skilled man saw things a lot differently compared to TGWU officials, which did not make for very good relationships. He was in favour of a national agreement as were some of our other senior stewards who wanted to sit 'at the top table'. I have already mentioned I was not then and never have been in favour of large organisations if they diminish the role of ordinary people.

Later on with negotiations moving towards a national grade structure, I proposed a different structure, which divided the whole Company into regions. I suggested that the Oxford and Swindon plants should be in the South East Region and that pay should be based on productivity and profits within the region. When I presented my proposal to the national negotiating committee it was not only rejected by all the craft unions, but also by Grenville Hawley and some of the TGWU senior stewards from plants in the UK other than Oxford.

I warned Hawley and others that if parity were achieved, there would be a widening of differentials between skilled and semi-skilled employees, a result many of us could not accept.

In 1978, after many many months of negotiations with neither side giving way, a national ballot was eventually held by the management on 'Parity Pay' for all manual employees and it was carried with 48,702, (65.72%) voting for and 25.403 (34.27%) against. It was a decision many semi-skilled workers who voted in favour came to regret.

Between 1971 and 1981 real wages for the semi-skilled production workers declined by 73.2% and for skilled men by 34%. This was the cause of real shop-floor resentment and my worst fears about the differentials between skilled and semi-skilled employees being changed in favour of skilled men were realised.

In August 1976 all national, regional and district officials from the TGWU and the AEU were summoned to an urgent special meeting at the TUC headquarters with Jack Jones, General Secretary of the TGW, and Hugh Scanlon, President of the

AEU, about the financial and industrial relations crisis in BL. At the start of the meeting Jack said the meeting could only last for one hour. They both said they had come straight from a meeting with the Prime Minister, Jim Callaghan, who had said the Government would not make any more capital available to BL until he knew that the serious disputes situation was brought under control. Within an hour Jones and Scanlon wanted to hear from each of us what we were going to do about the militant shop stewards who were causing so much trouble for the Company. Bearing in mind both Jones and Scanlon had constantly told us that full-time officials were to do as the shop stewards required, we reminded them that they had a share of the blame. A meeting, which should have lasted one hour, ended after four hours with everyone saying they would in future take a tougher line with militant stewards, providing we would have our unions' full support, which was given by both General Secretaries.

Early in 1977 Bill Thompson, the full-time official responsible for TGWU members in the Assembly Plant, announced his intention to retire. The question arose as to who should replace him - not an easy decision in view of the fact that our senior and deputy senior shop stewards were involved in an ideological fight not only with their employer but with their union as well. As I have said elsewhere, they were determined to operate a union within a union and continue with constant disputes causing serious differences of opinion among our members. My immediate thoughts about Bill Thompson's successor were therefore, "God help anyone who gets that job".

During August 1977 I received a message from the General Secretary's office saying Jack Jones and Harry Urwin, the Deputy General Secretary, would be visiting Oxford and wished to see me on an 'important matter'. A date was fixed and we met over dinner in an Oxford hotel. Jack Jones wasted no time in telling me what he had in mind. He said that the next official in the Assembly Plant would have to be someone who had the members' and the union's interests at heart and would be prepared to take on anyone who believed otherwise. He said that as I had proved myself in the Body Plant and had worked in the industry on the shop floor for fourteen years, nine as a shop steward and later as full-time official, he would like me to become responsible for all TGWU members in both plants, plus the other car industry companies. This meant members in Unipart, MG, Morris Radiators in North Oxford plus all twelve car-delivery firms.

Having known for several months that Bill Thompson wanted to retire this made me think that maybe I would be asked to take on such a huge responsibility. I was therefore ready with my response to Jack's question. I said I was willing to do as he asked provided I had his full support when I set about reorganising the two branches that were at war with one another in the Assembly Plant and ensuring that the union became an effective organisation, committed to our union's policies and the members' interests. I also said that I would do whatever it took to restore some order in our organisation within the plant. It would mean that I would face up to the extremists who included the senior shop steward and his deputies.

Jack replied, "As long as you carry out the policy of our union, do nothing illegal and comply with the union's rule book (this refers to election of stewards, etc.), you will have my full support". With that assurance, I agreed to his proposal that I would be responsible for all TGWU members involved in the Oxford car industry.

The following years brought me into some ferocious battles with the extremists, but Jack never once went back on his word.

Early struggles with the militants in the Assembly Plant

Once I had taken over the membership in the Assembly Plant the militants began campaigning for my removal. On one occasion, the Senior Shop Steward, Bob Fryer, who seemed to go along with the militants (maybe for an easier life) told me I was not allowed to enter the plant unless I had his permission. I told him in no uncertain terms that my job was to represent all members in the factory regardless of their political opinions and whilst I would never enter the plant without his knowledge, I would not seek his permission.

Several months after I had become responsible for the Assembly Plant, Jack Jones told me he had received many written motions proposed and passed by the militants' branch, plus several delegations of senior and deputy senior stewards to his office in London, demanding that I be sacked. He also told me that at one meeting a delegation of militants were so angry at his refusal to sack me, they poured a jug of water over him.

Attending meetings of shop stewards was often a nightmare. The militant stewards always made sure that they were at the front and they constantly heckled me with the aim of breaking up the meeting before I could give a report or make recommendations. On one occasion even chairs were being thrown at the platform to drive me off.

On another occasion a senior personnel manager phoned me to say there had been a serious skirmish following a mass meeting and that a shop steward had fled the meeting and hidden in a van. Someone found out where he was and lit a fire under the van. Fortunately it was soon put out with no harm done. As the result of the meeting was inconclusive, I was asked if I would come to the plant to sort things out. I didn't ring the senior steward to say I was on my way because I knew what the response would be. When I arrived in the personnel department I asked the Company to send for our senior steward.

When he arrived and saw me, he demanded to know why I had come to the plant without his permission. I replied, "I am here to deal with the problem you have been handling so sit down and tell me what the problem is". After two hours of negotiations we managed to solve the problem with no further trouble.

One of the ways of obtaining a strike was by militant stewards calling a meeting of a small section within the plant, which, if it stopped work, would affect a large number of workers and have a much wider effect. Having discussed an issue with the members, they would be told to vote for a strike. If the meeting was split for and against, stewards conducting the meeting told those members who were against the strike to go back to work. A second vote was called for all those in favour of striking. With a vote in favour, the management were informed of the decision and told that any work done by employees who had returned to work was "black" and would not be worked on.

Another example of industrial trouble was about a Deputy Senior Steward, Alan Thornett, who became known as "The Mole" by the media because he managed to keep his extremism under cover for a considerable time. Thornett was shop steward for the heavy goods drivers - crucial to the continued running of the plant. He would call a meeting of members and ask them to show by way of raising their hands, "All those in favour of a pay rise, please show". With a unanimous 'yes' vote this would be taken to the management and tabled as a claim. If a 'failure to agree' was reached the next stage in the disputes procedure was to call me in to further the claim. Very often I had no real case worth putting and members were told by Thornett that their union official was not capable of looking after their interests and they should therefore go on strike.

In one year I had to deal with five hundred strikes and one thousand pay claims from many parts of the plant. Many of the strikes and pay claims were linked. Some strikes lasted for no more than ten minutes; others could be anything up to three weeks. None were ever made official by our union.

When I asked Thornett why he and other militant stewards constantly made pay demands, which could not be met and only frustrated our members, he replied, "Because the workers must go down to one defeat after another until they learn to become revolutionaries."

I replied, "I am not here to give management victories at our members' expense". I also said I would make sure our members knew what he had said. This threat caused him to refrain from such practices from then on. I also warned the militants that if they continued to cause unnecessary disruption there was a risk that a more hard-line management would arrive.

When the opportunity arose for election of senior and deputy senior stewards, I suggested and implemented a system of secret ballots as our rule book permitted. I also decided to introduce a major change in how the election should be run, with every member having the right to a secret vote, as the existing system was one of self perpetuation where the senior shop steward and his deputies were elected by the shop stewards and not by the wider membership.

When I informed the senior shop steward and his deputies of my intended changes, they thought they would be running the election. At that time I did not tell them of my plans about who would run the election because I knew there would be a major campaign against me by the militants. I also insisted that every candidate must be nominated and seconded with many other provisions for a proper and fair election. My days as a parliamentary candidate in a general election stood me in good stead for running elections.

On polling day the militants were surprised when I brought into the Assembly Plant thirty-five shop stewards from other firms to run the whole election. That did not endear me to them. At the end of each shift, all the ballot boxes were locked up and guarded by the works' police until the count was held. All the candidates were allowed to be present during the count, but not allowed to handle any ballot papers. When the result was announced, the senior shop steward was defeated as were some of the militant deputies.

That was the end of a self-perpetuating system of elections in the plant. It did not prevent militant stewards being elected or disputes continuing, but it did introduce an element of democracy for all members, which they had not previously enjoyed.

The arrival of Michael Edwardes and a climate of fear

My prediction in 1997 of a hard-line management came true with the support of not only the Prime Minister, Mrs. Thatcher, but also the National Enterprise Board and the National Trade

Union leaders. It soon became clear we were to be confronted with a management that would brook no opposition and did not believe in winning hearts and minds for the betterment of the Company or its employees.

One of Edwardes' first acts was to call a huge meeting of senior managers, national, regional and district union officials and senior shop stewards at a hotel near Kenilworth, Warwickshire. Whilst I did not keep my notes of the meeting, I well remember him saying the Company would be managed very differently from in the past. He also promised he would bring an end to shop floor disruptions. Edwardes admitted he knew nothing about car making, having come from the Chloride Company, which made batteries. By a strange coincidence, I had been invited and gave a lecture there on 'Employee Participation and Productivity' several months before Edwardes left there to become Chairman of BL. I have often wondered if he ever knew I had given a talk to his senior managers and trade union representatives on such a subject.

After a brief time for questions, Derek Robinson, the Senior AEU Steward at Longbridge (known as Red Robbo) proposed a vote of thanks to Edwardes and a promise of the union's full support. There was a massive vote of thanks with the exception of five hands (one of them mine) that voted against Robinson's Motion. I voted against supporting Edwardes because I believed and, dare I say I think I was proved right, that we were to be confronted with a born autocrat who believed in authoritarianism not management with any form of consensus or mutual agreements. All the thanks Robinson got was being sacked in 1980 by Edwardes for urging resistance to closures arising from his Recovery Plan.

Whilst I might agree with Edwardes about the militants, I had different ideas about how to deal with them. I believed we should persuade the vast majority of members it was not in their best interests to elect such people because they were not loyal to their union or their employer and were using members for their political aims.

I once described Edwardes as an 'Industrial Thatcherite'. We soon found out his real intentions because a whole new group of managers came into the Company who had a total disregard for any local agreements and nothing but contempt for trade union representatives - shop stewards or full-time officials. Comments such as, "I wonder which stones they found these people under" were common among union officials and shop stewards. The shop floor was constantly flooded with Company literature designed to put the Company view of why they were pursuing a hard line towards their employees. Trade unions totally failed to match the propaganda campaign run by the management.

Both plants at Cowley felt the lash, as I did of Edwardes very early on. I remember on one occasion I had to go into the Assembly Plant over a strike when employees had refused to work in a flooded shop floor. It soon became obvious to me that the Personnel Manager, new to the plant, had no idea what the real problem was. When I asked him to come down onto the shop floor and see for himself, he agreed. On arrival in the area and in no time he said, "I now understand the problem" and agreed the men had no alternative but to stop work because of a dangerous situation working in water and handling electrical equipment. He also told me he had only been in the factory for six months and never had the time to visit the production lines.

On another occasion I was involved in a discussion with a manager in the Body Plant and found it necessary to say he should read the agreement I claimed the Company had broken. I had my copy with me and was quoting from it. He replied, "I wish I could read it but my predecessor took it with him". I discovered this was because personnel managers were not allowed to stay in one plant too long in case they became friendly with senior stewards and full-time officials and his predecessor had taken his copy with him when he was moved to another plant.

One day I received a phone call from a shop steward in the Body Plant to say that Bill Roche, our much respected senior shop steward, was about to be sacked for making derogatory remarks whilst addressing a mass meeting about the hard-line management we were now experiencing. The remarks were made when he asked men to return to work after they had gone on strike over the way they were being treated. Bill did not know a local press reporter was present at the back of the meeting who then reported what he had heard in the *Oxford Mail*. He was reprimanded by the Company and faced the possibility of being sacked. I immediately phoned the Senior Personnel Manager (an old Pressed Steel man) and requested a formal meeting to try and resolve the matter. The Personnel Manager was a person I knew well and had had dealings with over several years. We had hardly got started when the door burst open and the Production Manager, Ron Savage, (appropriately named) turned to the Personnel Manager and said, "What are you doing wasting Company time on bastards like these?" pointing to us. "Get off your arse and do something useful."

When I remonstrated with him and said it was a formal meeting and would he please leave, he replied, "And you can f*** off, you useless bastard." I asked for an apology but was refused.

I told him, "If you don't apologise I will leave the plant as you suggest and take all our members with me until you do". To his credit the Personnel Manager apologised for the Company after Savage had gone and said, "I am afraid that's the type of manager we are now employing."

It was not uncommon for people like Savage to swear constantly to shop stewards as a form of intimidation. A climate of fear was being used as a management tool. To be fair, many line managers were also under severe pressure to achieve their daily production targets. Shop stewards told me that many of them produced reports at the end of the shift saying they had met their production targets even if they had not, such was the fear they also felt.

Major events at the national level of the Company began to be felt both by unions and local plants. The Company decided to accept two important recommendations from the Ryder Report. The first was a proposal to move from fifty-eight bargaining units to one for all manual workers, both skilled and semi-skilled. This involved the formation of the BL National Negotiating Committee on which senior stewards and some local officials served. It was one of my misfortunes to be one of the local officials; misfortune because I never thought that genuine bargaining ever took place. The management, in the main, talked at us and not to us with some meetings lasting until 10 p.m. By the next morning each employee was handed a leaflet printed by the Company setting out what their view was of the meeting and any offers they had made.

Despite my trying endlessly to form a small group of our side to remain behind and follow the management's example of printing our view of what had been agreed or not, I was told it was the senior steward's job to hold a mass meeting at each plant and put our point of view to members, which did not require our view being put in writing.

The second Ryder proposal was to set up a National Participation Committee consisting of very senior management, including Michael Edwardes, and senior shop stewards. Bill Roche was its secretary. No national or local full-time officials were allowed to be members. This was a wonderful idea, which never worked out in practice because the Company had their ideas as to what needed to be done and did not take kindly to any opposition or genuine participation.

There were further problems, which caused severe difficulties to the senior shop stewards on the Participation Committee because they were told that everything discussed was strictly confidential and must not be reported to their members. This brought about a farcical situation between Bill Roche, our Senior Steward in the Body Plant, who was also joint secretary with a management representative on the committee.

A good example was an occasion when Bill Roche asked me to attend a disputes meeting in the Body Plant because several stewards were in dispute over changes the Company wanted to impose on working practices without either discussion or negotiation. Having prepared a reference for the meeting with management and a briefing from Bill, we agreed the case we intended to present to the Company. Having put the case that Bill and I had agreed, what I could not understand was the immediate response we received from the Company. They looked very surprised at what I had said and asked for a short adjournment.

Later a senior manager asked me to leave the meeting as he wished to tell me something important on my own. I would never meet management without Bill knowing and being present. When I told Bill what they wanted, Bill said, "Go ahead, I have no objections".

I returned to the manager who said, "I cannot understand why Bill Roche is supporting this reference as he knows the policy we are implementing has been agreed by the Participation Committee".

When I told Bill what I had been told and asked for an explanation he said, "He is right but I am sworn to secrecy about what happens at the Participation Committee meetings."

I said, "Well I'm not and I think the stewards have a good case so I intend to continue arguing for it".

Needless to say we got nowhere but it proved to me the Company did not have a genuine participation policy and never intended to have one or to try to meet trade union proposals, however good they were, if they conflicted with what the Participation Committee had agreed.

Negotiations at national level were proving more and more difficult for both sides. Management were failing to persuade the trade union side to accept their arbitrary style of management and the union side often could not agree what policies to pursue because each union had different policies based on the needs of their skilled and semi-skilled members.

By the end of the seventies both sides agreed to hold national ballots on major issues. There were five altogether between October 1977 and February 1980.

Management held a ballot on the intention to reform the bargaining process, which they won against our wishes. The second, run by the unions, was against the Company's proposals for a company-wide incentive scheme, which we won. The third, on the Company's proposal seeking support for 'Pay Parity' throughout the Company for all manual employees, was won by the Company against TGWU advice. The fourth was run by the Company on the Edwardes recovery plan. This was the only ballot to include white-collar employees as well as manual, which the Company won.

The 1980 ballot was run by the Confederation of Ship Builders and Engineering Unions (Confed) on behalf of the BL unions asking the members to reject the 1979/1980 pay offer, which the unions won.

When we told the Company on the national negotiating committee of our intention to hold a ballot on their offer, they said they were pleased to hear that.

As the national officials said nothing I asked the management that if their offer was rejected would they honour the ballot result and return to the bargaining table for further negotiations. They replied, "Certainly not, what is on the table is our final offer". It was at that moment that the unions realised the Company would not commit themselves to honouring ballot results if they lost and felt it important enough to ignore it.

To a certain extent I understood their reaction because if they had agreed to accept the result from a ballot, all votes against an offer could be endless until the union side obtained what they wanted.

The Company brought balloting into disrepute because even when they agreed the unions would hold a ballot, or they held one, if the result did not suit them, they ignored the result anyway and imposed the changes they wanted or refused to honour union ballot results.

This issue raises the important questions of which matters should be resolved by the use of ballots and which should not, and why.

Chapter 5

The slow decline begins.
Closure of MG, Abingdon

MG carnival parade through Abingdon in September 1979

The MG Car Company held a carnival in Abingdon in September 1979 to celebrate fifty years of production in the town. The procession consisted of many floats and models of cars, which had been produced over the fifty years, some being driven, others on the back of lorries. In the evening a civic reception was held as part of the anniversary celebrations at which the Plant Director, Peter Frearson, thanked the Mayor for the Town Council's support over fifty years. During the toast to the Town and MG's future, Frearson said, "On to the next fifty years." The following Monday he received a phone call from BL's headquarters telling him to announce the closure of the plant within three months. I understand there had been no prior warning of what was to come. The stewards began a publicity campaign to save the plant and their jobs and let the public know what was happening to this much-respected car factory and the people who made it.

The management tried to stop the campaign by saying that anyone who did anything to prevent the closure would be dismissed due to industrial misconduct and would lose all their entitlements including severance pay. The campaign against closure collapsed and the final irony was that each employee received a letter of thanks for 'assisting the Company in closing the plant down'. This was another good example of the new breed of management we could expect in the future.

Members asked their unions to get involved and see what could be done to change the management's mind. Having met the management it became clear there was no chance of anyone having the authority to change the decision. We decided to do two things. Firstly to go straight into the disputes procedure and if that failed, which it did, take the Company to the Central Arbitration Committee (CAC), a procedure within the Employment Protection Act 1975, on the grounds that the unions were being denied the real reasons to close the plant. The AEU were also involved and it was agreed I should do the presentation to the CAC on behalf of our two unions.

In view of the importance of the subject, the Tribunal was held on the 18th January 1980 in London where I presented our case and tabled fifteen detailed questions about information we required. During the hearing the management side said they were prepared to discuss the effects of their decision to close the plant but not negotiate the decision or tell us why.

In April 1980 the Tribunal decided that:

> In the face of refusal by the management to bargain, the unions cannot exercise their statutory right to bargain for information. We emphasise our conclusion that this is a situation in which the management has a moral obligation to bargain. If at any time the management concedes that point it will be necessary to decide how much of the information sought is within the contemplation of the statutory obligation.

On that technical and procedural point, the Tribunal found against us. The Company never came back to us with a willingness to provide their reasons for the closure. We always thought it was an instruction by the Government, which they didn't want to reveal. Peter Frearson left the Company and the UK in disgust at the way he and all the employees had been treated. I understand he went to manage a car plant in Malaysia.

The closure of MG and the demolition of the plant was a microcosm of the Government's policy in the 1980s of moving away from manufacturing to financial services, which many workers could not understand. The MG site is now a huge housing estate, with a retail park close by, selling goods made in the Far East. This means the area is now selling imported goods rather than earning foreign revenue for the UK from exports.

My meeting with Michael Edwardes

I had become so angry at the authoritarian methods used by Edwardes and what I regarded as the worst type of management on the shop floor that I started writing to the national media and agreed to do interviews on radio and TV about my concerns. As a result, many well-known Labour correspondents in most national newspapers were contacting me on an almost daily basis for news about BL and Cowley in particular.

In addition I was invited to give TV interviews for German and French TV about Cowley. A letter I sent to *The Guardian*, which they kindly published in July 1980, criticised Edwardes and his style of management. My letter was in response to an article John Torode had written about BL's industrial scene. In it he said,

> Edwardes sees the need for a more active and aggressive management style and far greater involvement by line management - from the foreman up through to plant director and the company chairman.

The whole article with quotes from senior directors gave the impression that BL had tamed the unions through tough management.

Pat Lowry, the Company's Personnel Director even claimed in one article, "We have made ballots respectable."

My letter to *The Guardian* prompted Edwardes to write to me complaining that I was unhelpful to all he was trying to achieve in BL. He even mentioned that, "National unions saw the need to close ranks at this PERILOUS time, I regret that you don't." He concluded his letter with an invitation that if I would like to debate this matter privately, to let him know and a meeting could be arranged. Needless to say I jumped at the chance, as it was most unusual for a man in his position to bother about local union officials and their views. Also, I wanted to tell him to his face what I thought about his style of management and his contempt for workers' rights in the pursuit of economic success. I phoned his secretary to say I would welcome an opportunity to meet him and asked for a suggested date. By a strange coincidence she suggested the 11th August - my birthday. I said that I would rather spend the day with my family than meet Edwardes but if that was the only day he could do I agreed to come to his office in London at 4 p.m. on the 11th of August 1980.

When I arrived I was sitting in the reception room for Edwardes' guests when Pat Lowry passed by. He seemed very surprised at seeing me and asked, "What brings you here David?" I told him I had been invited by Edwardes and he said, "Good luck with Napoleon." I was then ushered into Edwardes office suite by his secretary who showed me where to sit and said that he would soon be joining me.

Edwardes began the meeting by exploding on me, accusing me of doing him and the Company damage by my letter in *The Guardian* and other criticisms in the media. It lasted for about ten minutes. Not a good start from him, bearing in mind my problems with militants in the assembly plant. I let him continue without interruption and waited for him to finish. When he fell silent I said, "Mr. Edwardes I am not afraid of you like most of your managers. I have not come here to have a bollocking, but to discuss with you your style of management and contempt for workers' rights."

He replied, "Do you have an agenda then?"

I replied, "I have. These are items I would like to discuss with you:

    a)   Your style of management

    b)   Your refusal to honour the management/union run ballot results when the Company lost.

    c)   The closure of the MG Car Plant at Abingdon.

On the first two we had about thirty minutes of discussion but simply could not agree when he said it was essential in the interests of the Company and the Government that BL required a strong leadership to bring things round, which required making difficult decisions. When I said that economic success should not be obtained at the expense of human rights on the shop floor, he looked surprised at my comment and clearly did not agree.

With regard to the MG closure he said the plant was not successful and like many other plants had to be shut down. I set out the reasons why the workers and local management were so angry at the reason and the haste of which the closure was announced two days after the 50th Anniversary celebration. He replied, "Mr Buckle you have your boss in Transport House (meaning our General Secretary), mine is in Number 10." To be fair to Edwardes, I assumed he was referring to the fact that BL was in public ownership and he had to obey politician's orders. At that point the discussion ended.

As I was about to leave, his secretary entered the room carrying a tray with a birthday cake and a pot of tea. Edwardes said, "I understand it's your birthday, please accept this cake as a present."

I declined saying, "Thank you but I don't want to leave this office with a cake under my arm." Industrial psychology was not Edwardes' strong point! He didn't seem to realise that what crossed my mind was that it might be put round BL that I was sent packing with a birthday cake. I agree this may seem churlish, but that was the atmosphere in BL in those days.

During the latter part of 1979 the Company began a campaign to end our 'Mutuality agreement' plus other employee entitlements, which they saw as a challenge to their right to manage.'

1980 and 1981 proved as traumatic and turbulent as the previous decades but for different reasons.

On the 25th March 1980 the Company informed employees that anyone who reported for work on the 8th and 9th of April was deemed to have accepted a major change in their employment conditions. Anyone who failed to report for work would be deemed to have dismissed himself. This amounted to an unacceptable imposition of the worst kind, but how very typical of the worst kind of authoritarian management.

Our members had to accept the new conditions or lose their jobs, which included an imposition by the management of a new grade structure, new grade rates, totally different working practices, which ended 'Mutuality', and an incentive pay scheme, which employees had voted against in a Company-wide ballot by 46,107 against and only 21,759 for. The imposition of these new conditions did nothing to improve industrial relations and disputes once again reared their head even in the Body Plant, which had enjoyed many years of industrial peace and mutual agreements between management and employees on the production lines.

Introduction of national pay negotiations

My worst fears were realised following the formation of the National Negotiating Committee (NNC). It was my misfortune to be a member and see what happened at first hand. The NNC meant the end of all local negotiations and involved union representatives attending endless meetings with shop stewards from all over the UK, plus even more meetings with senior management. The great advantage for management and national union leaders meant that bargaining was taken out of the hands of local officials and senior shop stewards. Both senior management and national union officials took full advantage of the new set up to our disadvantage.

The 1980 pay negotiations took ages and nearly ended with a strike but in the end the membership rejected the advice of their negotiating team and reluctantly accepted the Company's offer. The 1981 negotiations turned into a farce, which is well worth recording for those who are interested in BL and, in particular, how not to resolve industrial relations problems.

Having failed to reach an agreement within the NNC, a national strike was decided by our members to record their objections to the Company's offer, which it was not prepared to improve. Eventually, after many more days of negotiations, it was agreed by both sides to refer the matter to the Advisory Conciliation and Arbitration Service (ACAS) to help resolve the matter. Neither side wanted arbitration. We all went to the ACAS headquarters' office in London on a November Saturday morning in 1981.

The day began with Michael Edwardes going on national radio saying he had been in touch with a senior government minister who gave him the authority to say that if the meeting failed to reach an agreement the Company would be wound up. This was not the first time he had made such threats. If the unions had made similar remarks the Company would have said they were not prepared to negotiate under duress.

When we arrived at the ACAS headquarters we were greeted by none other than Pat Lowry, then Chairman of ACAS but who only recently had been BL's top personnel manager. Lowry was the architect of the very policy we were objecting to, so by no stretch of the imagination could he be described as unbiased. Our objections to him conducting the day's negotiations fell on deaf ears.

ACAS provided four rooms for both sides. Senior BL managers were in one, junior managers in another. The national unions' leaders were in another room and we local officials and senior stewards in the fourth room. ACAS officials, as we learnt after some time, were flitting between the other three rooms, leaving us sidelined. Lowry was a skilled operator in this kind of situation. It was not my idea of genuine collective bargaining or effective communications between management and unions. None of the union leaders consulted us during the morning.

At mid-day we demanded that Alex Kitson, our Union's Assistant General Secretary, come to our room and tell us what was going on. The first thing we told him was that our General Secretary, Moss Evans, had assured us we would be involved in all the final negotiations. We then asked what, if any, negotiations had taken place and how far they had got and why we were not involved. His reply in a strong Scottish accent was, "We're no' negotiating, brothers, just sounding each other out." We believed him and asked him to keep us informed and bring us in when the negotiations began.

Evans agreed to our request and assured us that the national officials of all the unions would not negotiate or reach any agreement without us being involved. We were not convinced, but accepted what he said. At about 10.30 p.m. we were informed that ACAS would be holding a special meeting in the main hall at which all the parties would be invited to attend.

When we arrived at the conference hall all the general secretaries and national union officials were there including, to our surprise, Len Murray, the General Secretary of the TUC who chaired the meeting. His opening remarks were, "I wish to report what has been agreed with the management during a day of long and difficult negotiations."

We protested in vain about how we had been excluded from any meetings during the day. We were even more angered by John Boyd of the AEU telling us we must go back to our districts and hold mass meetings before Sunday night, when a company-wide strike was due to take place, and tell our members to accept the Company's pay offer of 3.8%, which had been agreed by national officials.

The agreed formula was handed to us and, having read it, a senior steward asked Len Murray if anything could be added or if there could be further negotiations with us being involved. Murray replied, "No." I then asked Murray if we could reject any part of the agreement. I had in mind rejecting the whole lot. Murray again said "No" and that we were 'at the end of the line'. National officials had given in to Edwardes' blackmail and threats of closing the Company down and there was nothing we could do about it. The instructions from the national trade union leaders were that we must inform members a deal had been agreed.

We returned to our districts and held mass meetings on Monday morning putting as brave a face as we could when reporting what had happened. Members and local union officials knew that if the national union officials were in support of the Company's offer there was no chance of an official strike. I asked Moss Evans to come to Oxford so he could meet the membership himself and see their expected anger. He declined the invitation.

The whole experience proved one thing to me - national bargaining was a farce and undemocratic when employers like BL were involved. It also serves the interests of national union leaders because it avoids them having to pay strike pay in such circumstances and even more importantly general secretaries retain control over their members' aspirations.

Just before the end of Edwardes' five-year appointment was reached, he flew to Japan to complete a deal with Honda to produce a new car model, later named the Triumph Acclaim. It turned out to be one of his better decisions as it provided much needed work for Cowley.

The author overlooking the Car Plant in August 1982.
Photograph courtesy of the *Financial Times*.

Later on when I was advised that Honda technicians would be coming to Cowley to supervise work on the production lines, I suggested that the Company should make it known what they were planning and find out if anyone was an ex Japanese prisoner-of-war who might not want to be anywhere near them or work under their direction. They accepted my advice and discovered there were 28 people. Each of them was informed of what was being planned and luckily no one complained.

Several months later we were informed that the first car parts of the new model would be arriving in crates from Southampton docks. I asked the shop stewards to keep me informed as to what the parts would be like. To my pleasant surprise I received a phone call saying the crates had arrived. The foreman gave the workers crowbars and hammers to break open the crates and remove the parts. I was told that as the crates were so well made the workers refused to damage them and opened them very carefully. When I asked, "What about the quality of the parts?"

I was told, "They actually fit first time."

The point about parts fitting first time is very important so far as line speeds and productivity are concerned. Earlier I mentioned the three huge press shops stamping out various car panels. Due to lack of investment in the 1950s and 1960s the dies in the presses, which turn a piece of flat metal into a shape were grossly over used and needed to be thoroughly overhauled or scrapped and replaced after 100,000 stampings. Dies in the press shops were used for up to 500,000 stampings. Such over use of a die meant that 20% of all stampings had to be scrapped. It also meant that in the case of door panels, it was not unusual for men to make the doors fit with a rawhide mallet. There was a time when the Hillman Minx, Rover and Rolls Royce car bodies all had large amounts of molten lead loaded on to the seams to cover design faults. Having been loaded on, the lead soon hardened and the line worker had to disc two thirds of it off to obtain a smooth surface. This explains why so many workers had to be regularly checked for lead poisoning and why there was so much fine lead dust in the atmosphere and on the shop floor.

One other comment members made was that they could not understand why a British Prime Minister, who claimed to be very patriotic was allowing foreign manufacturers such as Nissan, Toyota and Honda to build factories in the UK at the expense of British-made cars and appeared not to want to ensure the survival of BL. Workers from MG, for understandable reasons, expressed this view much more strongly than Cowley workers.

One interesting by-product of the Honda deal was a call I had from a Japanese Professor, Hiedo Totsuka from Tokyo University, who said he was coming to Britain and wanted to see me. My initial thoughts were that he might well be an advance party on behalf of Honda to sound unions out about possible problems with Cowley employees not wanting to produce Japanese cars and how their technicians should relate to line workers. I agreed to meet him and we soon struck up a good working relationship after he assured me he had nothing to do with Honda but was only interested in the British car industry as he was carrying out a comparative study of British and Japanese car manufacturers and of any industrial relations problems. I assured him he had come to the right place if it was difficult industrial relations problems he was interested in.

It turned out that his main concern was how much Japanese management control over British workers on production lines would be acceptable to them. This took us into a very interesting conversation about 'Mutuality' and employee participation - not a subject very dear to Japanese car companies. As a result of our discussions he came back to the UK on several occasions each time wanting to meet me for further discussions.

On one visit he recorded an interview of me expanding my views on the subject of worker participation and 'Mutuality' for his students. On his return he informed me that many students, plus employees of Toyota, were very interested and wanted to try and obtain similar rights in their Company. Nissan workers thought participation was a denial of management rights and wanted none of it. Eventually Tokyo University published a book with my views on employee participation, each page having two columns, one in Japanese and the other with an English translation. I would be interested to know if there are any employees enjoying 'Mutuality' or employee's participation in any Japanese car factories. I very much doubt it!

Edwardes leaves after five years as Chairman

Whilst they dare not come out in the open and admit it, many junior and senior managers were glad to see the back of Edwardes, as they had also experienced a hard time keeping up with his authoritarian methods. When he took over the Company in November 1977 he said he 'knew nothing about making cars but he would do his best'. I would say he proved that, during his time at BL, but what he also proved to most people was that his style of management did not allow for winning the hearts and minds of employees to get the best out of them for the Company's sake and their own. By the end of his time he had reduced the workforce from 198,000 to 90,000, and of thirty-four plants he had closed fourteen. Production had been halved even though new models had been launched. BL's market share in Britain was below 15% and it had an even smaller share of export markets. Edwardes may have known nothing about making cars but he scarcely demonstrated much more knowledge of the secret of success.

Early in 1983 Edwardes published his book, *Back from the Brink* telling his side of the story of the problems he faced managing BL. Whilst there was much I did agree with, there was also a lot I profoundly disagreed with, especially when he sought to justify his policy of hard line management as the only way to pull the Company round. Edwardes saw any opposition, whether good or bad as a challenge to his right to manage. He said, "We needed to re-establish management authority."

The magazine *New Socialist* invited me to review his book, which they published in August 1983. I reminded readers of his style of management and said:

> The Company expects, and rightly so, a high quality product. The employees are equally entitled to a quality of life. My real criticism of the Edwardes' era is that he put commercial success far above human needs, but surely there has to be a balance struck. If not, modern industry is turning people into robots, and no one should complain if they revolt. Edwardes may have thought the crisis he inherited justified an authoritarian industrial relations system, but a different style is required now - more open, trusting and democratic.

When Harold Musgrove took over from Michael Edwardes it seemed to me that he wanted to run the Company on the same lines as his predecessor. Musgrove introduced a system on the production lines called 'Zones of control.' Production lines were divided up into sections with huge notices giving each section a number. Workers and shop stewards were instructed not to tell any employees in another section what had happened in their section and to leave the plant without talking to anyone on the way out. Shop stewards saw this as dividing the union rep's and making it very difficult, if not impossible, to co-ordinate any union activity. Despite my presentations to management about the new system, it made no difference. I was told, "We are determined to control what goes on each day and will brook no interference with how we manage the lines." 'Mutuality' was anathema to the management!

After two years, Musgrove was replaced by Graham Day who had been running the loss making British Shipbuilding. Day described himself as, 'a hard working professional manager'. He was reported as saying he knew nothing about making cars (it reminded me that Edwardes had said the same), but selling cars was much the same as selling shoes. Those comments by the incoming Chairman of BL endeared him to no one. The one good thing he did was to set up a marketing department, which amazingly BL lacked. It was also reported that early on in his role as Chairman of BL he clashed with some senior executives because of their 'pseudo-macho culture' in the upper reaches of the Company, which he felt inhibited discussions on what the Company should do. The very same point I made in my review of Edwardes' book.

It was not only Michael Edwardes I was glad to see the back of. One of the leading Trotskyites, Alan Thornett, was sacked for industrial misconduct in November 1982. What happened is worth recording because it tells readers a great deal about how both the Trots and management behave under certain circumstances.

When I was informed that Thornett had been sacked, I took immediate action and requested an urgent disputes procedure meeting with the management because I expected all the lorry drivers in the Assembly Plant to withdraw their labour in his support. A strike by drivers would have closed the whole plant down. I need not have worried because not one driver came out on strike in support of their shop steward throughout all the hearings, both in the factory and at the employment tribunal.

The Company alleged that Thornett had taken a day off work without permission or explanation. When he was challenged by management why, he said he had been 'sick'. However, the

71

Company found out he had gone to Nottingham to renew his HGV driver's licence, which was 4 years out of date. I represented him through the dismissal procedure saying that the Company were as much to blame as he was because it was their legal responsibility also to ensure drivers' licences were kept up to date.

Not being successful, I advised Thornett to apply to an industrial tribunal on the grounds the punishment was out of proportion to the alleged offence committed and therefore amounted to unfair dismissal. Normally a district official would represent a member at the tribunal. On this occasion I asked the union to provide legal assistance for Thornett, as I felt that despite my intense dislike for him because of the harm he had done to our union, he was still entitled to whatever service I and the union could provide. However, I was not prepared to represent him at a tribunal in view of the bad relationship I had with him. On those grounds I asked the union to provide Thornett with a barrister, which they agreed to. As a result he and I met the barrister in London when it was decided to request the Company to provide 'further and better particulars' about the actions they had taken prior to the dismissal procedure. They complied with our request and included, by mistake, a written instruction from a senior director directing local management to sack Thornett even before the disciplinary procedure had begun. That decision meant he would be sacked whatever representations were made on his behalf. On those grounds unfair dismissal was eventually accepted by BL and Thornett was offered £5000 but not reinstatement. He asked me to try and get more. When £8000 was offered, he refused, saying he was still not satisfied. This was from a man who had told members in the past, "Never sell your job to management under any circumstances, fight them."

When our barrister warned him it was a final offer and if he refused he might end up with nothing, he accepted £8000. We were about to go back into the tribunal and finalise matters when I noticed Thornett was missing. I mentioned this to our barrister, who replied, "We don't need him."

I said, "Oh yes we do and I would strongly advise you not to settle until Thornett is asked by you in front of the tribunal if he accepts BL's offer." I said that if he were not present when the settlement was agreed, he would claim that he had been 'sold down the river' by his union and the legal team, as the settlement had been made behind his back.

My advice was accepted and I was asked to find him and bring him back to face the tribunal. I eventually found him outside the building talking to a journalist from the left-wing *Workers Press Militant*. At first he refused to return. I said that if he didn't, the matter would be resolved without any settlement being made in his favour. On returning, our barrister asked him in front of the tribunal if he agreed to accept the £8,000 offer, and he replied, "Yes" and left. This did not stop him from claiming he had been 'victimized'. I, like many of our members, was glad to be rid of him, as I believe he was a greater danger to our members' job security than their employer. I have gone into some detail on this case to demonstrate the kind of problems our union faced with people whose loyalties lay elsewhere than their union and our members' interests. I cannot resist saying it also shows how the management couldn't even get rid of a dangerous militant efficiently as he left the Company with a victory over BL, plus £8,000.

Thornett's departure sadly didn't make a great deal of difference to disputes in the Assembly Plant but it did help to calm things down for a while. The culture of anti-management under any circumstances was surprisingly still very strong, even in 1982. It was due to the early history of the Company's refusal to recognise the right of employees to belong to a union and have recognition and genuine negotiating rights. This culture had become part of the life blood of the factory, unlike the Body Plant where, may I remind readers, trade union recognition had been obtained in 1936 so strikes and other disputes were much less likely.

The legacy of Edwardes' five years at BL was deep resentment and suspicion of management by not only the workforce but also among some of the line managers who could not agree with the orders they were given about how to treat employees, including removing rights, which had been in existence for many years known as 'custom and practice'. This was demonstrated during my last major dispute at the Assembly Plant, which involved the AEU as well as us.

Since 1946 workers had the right to wash their hands at the end of the morning and afternoon shifts. A senior director, visiting the plant one morning saw men leaving the production lines three minutes early at lunchtime. He gave an immediate order that the practice should be stopped at once. We tried through all the usual procedures to claim the right, as 'custom and practice' but the management were adamant it must stop. We were also told that when the workers reported for work on the following Monday they would be 'deemed to have accepted' that the six minutes washing up time had ceased and it was no longer a right. Both unions' officials warned senior members of management that if they insisted there would be a mass walkout of the employees. Our warning came true when 5,000 workers left the plant within thirty minutes.

The strike became known as the 'washing up dispute' and in our view symbolised the pent-up anger among the workers over the arbitrary decisions and actions of the management at all levels.

Once again negotiations were held at local and national level and became very difficult. Management were adamant they would not give way, as they saw that as a sign of weakness on their part and not how Edwardes would have dealt with the problem. In addition to the negotiations, both unions had decided to keep members informed of what was being said and done on their behalf. It was therefore decided that we would hold mass meetings on a local sports ground and that I would be the main speaker. This involved me in many meetings, one of which was to tell members that both unions had decided to make the strike official, a very unusual thing for the Assembly Plant.

The other strange event was the support I received at the mass meetings from the extremists who were always at the front of any meeting ready to shout me down. My line was that the Company deserved to find themselves in a serious strike situation, because this was entirely due to the way workers had been treated ever since Edwardes became Chairman of BL. To my embarrassment the Trots cheered the loudest. It was the one and only time they ever gave me any support.

At the height of the dispute I summed up the feelings of many BL employees by saying in an interview to the national press, "If the price of economic success is a system of industrial slavery, that is too high a price for working people to pay.' I used the word 'slavery' because I knew the media would ridicule the strike over workers wanting to wash their hands. The use of the word 'slavery' struck the right chord with the press, TV and radio because it gave me an opportunity in interviews to spell out what a harsh management employees were being confronted by. On the whole I felt we had a more sympathetic response by the media on why our members were on strike. The other issue members felt very strongly about was the Company's obvious contempt for a 'custom and practice', which had been in existence since the 1940s.

Eventually, local officials from both unions were instructed to attend a meeting in a hotel just outside Heathrow at which the directors of BL and two general secretaries, Moss Evans for the TGWU and Terry Duffy for the AEU were there in an effort to bring the dispute to an end. The meeting began at 4.00 p.m. and lasted until 8.00 a.m. the following morning, followed by a press conference and TV interviews.

The author - 8th April 1983
Photograph by Mark Ellidge,
courtesy of *The Sunday Times*

Once again as happened in ACAS, local officials and senior shop stewards were in one room, national union leaders in another and directors in another. We had no idea what was going on until about 2.30 a.m. when Evans and Duffy entered and said they were not making any progress and demanded that I produce a formula to 'resolve the dispute.' I told Moss I had done one and he had it in his possession. He said, "It's no good, write another one. I will be back in an hour and expect you to have it ready for me then." When I refused, saying I had nothing further to add, he threatened to sack me.

To my huge surprise, Bob Fryer who had been lining up with the Trots, (but never one in the true sense), said to Moss, "Don't treat our district secretary like that or you will have me and the rest of our members to deal with." Moss later apologised to me and let the matter drop. I later learned he was very ill and was clearly under a lot of stress as a result.

Both general secretaries continued along the lines of our formula and at 7.00 a.m. told us the Company would not pursue the issue for at least 6 months and then the right to have 6 minutes per day would be phased out. It never was. It was estimated by the Company that the strike cost BL £50m and that each member lost about £500 in wages.

Towards the end of the strike, Robert Taylor of the *Sunday Observer* wrote a profile, in which he quoted me saying:

> The Company is sitting on a three-legged stool. It has the finance to support them, good product plans but if it fails to achieve good human relations as well it will not succeed.

He continued by writing:

> This is not the language of the class war but Buckle is no 'Red Robbo'. Buckle is an articulate moderate. He is proving a more difficult man to deal with for BL than a militant left-winger, but whether he can force the Company to humanise its industrial relations policy remains to be seen.

In view of an authoritarian management, I continued with my criticism of them and took every opportunity to comment in the press, TV and radio, both nationally and locally.

To my surprise I began to receive invitations from many organisations, such as colleges in Oxford (Nuffield and Magdalen), the University of Warwick, the Industrial Society and several public schools including Radley College and Abingdon School, to give talks entitled *The BL Industrial Relations Situation* and *The Role of Trade Unions in a Modern Society*.

One invitation, which stands out in my mind, was from St. George's House Study Centre in Windsor Castle, under the direction of Michael Mann, Dean of Windsor Castle. I was invited to give a talk at a two-day seminar on the subject, *Coping with Conflict*. Having given the talk about conflict in BL and my struggles with militancy at the Assembly Plant, there followed a very interesting discussion about the dangers of militancy not only in the car industry but society generally.

In his summary of my talk and the discussion which followed, the Chairman, Michael Mann, commented that all militants were a 'great danger to society and should be removed from any situations of influence.' A member of the audience asked Michael Mann, "There was a Man called Jesus Christ who wanted to drive the money lenders out of the Temple and wanted to radically change society. Is the Dean suggesting that Jesus should also have been removed from society as He could also have been described as a dangerous militant?"

The Dean gave a reply, which amounted to, "There are exceptions to every rule."

Another interesting experience involved the Industrial Society, of which I had been a member of their Executive Council for several years. The Council consisted of senior industrialists and I as a trade unionist was an exception to the rule. The late John Garnett who recruited me was the Director and our Patron was the Duke of Edinburgh. The headquarters, which had been refurbished, were on The Mall, and the Duke was invited to open the new building. John Garnett informed each member of the Council that we would be introduced to the Duke for a brief chat on a one to one basis. When it came to my turn, Garnett introduced me to the Duke saying, "Mr Buckle is a trade union official responsible for the car industry in Oxford."

The Duke turned to me and said, "Are you responsible for all the strikes there?"

I replied, "I think it is a reasonable assumption by me that you have never worked in a car plant, may I tell you what it is like?" I then proceeded to describe working conditions at Cowley and the style of management, which caused so much resentment among many employees.

The Duke listened patiently and said, "Thank you. I am better informed now than when this conversation began." I just nodded my head and that was the end of our brief chat.

Writing about members of the Royalty reminds me of when I met the Duke of Kent in the BMW plant. At the time, in 1997, I was Chairman of the Oxfordshire County Council. Whenever a member of the Royal Family came to the County (other than private visits) it was the Chairman's job to be present and formally welcome them on behalf of the County. The Duke of Kent had been invited by BMW to visit the factory and I was there to meet him. As the Duke and a Plant Director and I were walking down one of the production lines, the Duke asked the Director, "What are industrial relations like now compared to the past?"

Before the Director could reply I said, "A lot better than when I worked here, because it is quieter, cleaner and safer, due to the massive investment by BMW (£1bn), which BL denied it in the past. The conditions you see now are what we begged for in the 1950s and 1960s but could not obtain."

At the height of the industrial trouble at Cowley in the seventies, the Head Master of Abingdon School, James Cobban, a fellow magistrate on the Abingdon Bench, invited me to give a talk to the upper sixth form on the subject, *The Role of Trade Unions in a Modern Society*. I welcomed the opportunity because I saw it as a challenge in an atmosphere where there may well have been hostility towards unions. Before going in to meet the boys, I was warned by the Head Master that one pupil in the audience was very hostile to unions and may well heckle me.

Having introduced me he turned to me and said, "David, the boys have been told not to interrupt you for the first twenty minutes of your talk, after that you are on your own."

I responded saying, "In the trade union movement we are not used to talking to captive audiences that are not allowed to respond. As far as I am concerned they are free from that restriction from now on." This was received with applause.

I only had one interruption and that came from the boy Cobban had warned me about. I had been explaining about the right of people to join a union of their choice in the West compared to Communist and Fascist countries where free unions do not exist. The boy I had been warned about shouted, "All trade unions should be banned everywhere", which received muted applause.

My reply was, "You are entitled to hold those views but what are you, a Communist or a Fascist?"

He was about to walk out when the Head Master said, "You interrupted the speaker, now answer his question." He mumbled a reply, which I could not hear.

In a quiet moment during questions Cobban said, "Whilst a boy thinks up a question, could you explain why there are nine unions in BL."

I replied, "Yes, Head Master, providing you explain why there are fourteen unions in the teaching profession." The boys greeted that with laughter.

After giving my explanation he gave his, saying, "As a matter of fact I will be attending the Annual Conference of my Association this weekend."

I took my opportunity to say to the boys, "Here we have it, we are both trade unionists." The meeting ended with laughter.

The Assembly Plant had its first strike free year in 1985, which was a relief to everyone and a major defeat for the militants.

In 1986 BL management, trade unions and members learnt with horror that the Government had been holding secret talks with the Ford Motor Company to take over BL. The first BL management knew about what was going on was when they were instructed to hand over all BL's commercial secrets to Ford, to enable them to make a careful assessment as to whether they could make a success of running BL. This so infuriated several BL directors that they offered their resignations. Despite my constant criticism of the way both the directors and the Government had treated BL, the directors were contacting me to see if there was anything the unions or I could do to put a stop to selling BL to Ford. They were even providing me with information about the representations they were making to the Cabinet. Directors who had seen me as their enemy in the past were now enlisting my support.

Ford, having learned BL's secrets, in particular their future model plans, decided, much to the anger of the government, not to make a bid for BL. The Government in 1988 then turned to British Aero Space (BAe) and asked them to take over BL. Their response was to say, "We are not in the car-making industry, we know nothing about it and do not wish to become involved." There were very strong rumours in BL that the Government told BAe that if they refused to take BL under their wing, it might influence future Government orders. It was alleged that the threat hanging over BAe made them decide that they would take over BL for only five years. Eventually BAe agreed and paid £150 million for the Company.

In July 1988 the Company announced closure of the Cowley South Works, followed in 1989 by the North Works' closure. At the end of that year I retired.

In April 1994 BMW bought what was then called the Rover Group for £850 million. Many of the remaining directors and senior managers of BL left the Company in disgust at the way they had been treated.

By 1992 the Assembly Plant had been closed completely and all car production concentrated in the Cowley Body Plant. The workforce was reduced to 4,500 compared to 14,000 in the 1960s/1970s. A vast area of wasteland existed for a time where the factory once stood and small business parks and light industries sprang up in their place - the same fate that engulfed the MG site! It is a microcosm of what befell so much of Britain's manufacturing industry during the 1980s.

If I were a cynic I would say the extremists were proud of the fact their objective of closing a plant down had been achieved. I make that comment because, in one of my arguments with a militant shop steward, I asked him what he hoped to achieve with so many strikes. He replied, "We must close the plant down, get rid of the management and hand the factory over to the workers."

Manufacturing which earned so much of Britain's bread and butter in the past has gone. No wonder we have a difficulty in getting out of the current financial crisis, because we no longer enjoy earnings from a strong manufacturing base like Germany.

Of all the lessons I learned from my experience as a production line worker, shop steward and full time union official the major one is this - if Governments restrict human rights they open the door to extremists. The same applies to employers who deny their employees the right to belong to an organisation of their choice such as unions, as William Morris did in the 1930s.

I have always believed management do not have a 'right to manage' - they have a 'duty to manage humanely.' A lesson neither William Morris nor BL management ever learnt.

Likewise, I always have believed and always will believe that official strikes are a legitimate weapon for workers to use in the face of injustice by Governments or employers, but must always be used as a last resort, not the first.

Much could be learned by many employers from the way the John Lewis Partnership is managed, the way its employees are treated and how it manages to win their hearts and minds.

Chapter 6

Visits to Germany and Russia
Part 1
Volkswagen car plant,
Wolfsburgh, Germany

My visit to the Volkswagen factory at Wolfsburg, West Germany, was a revelation compared to the Cowley factories.

During 1978 I had been assisting Peter Seglow a senior research fellow at Uxbridge University on a comparative study of the German and British car industry's industrial relations problems. To my surprise, he invited me to join with him and one of his colleagues on a visit to the Volkswagen plant in West Germany and also to West Berlin where he asked me to give a lecture to a small group of German industrialists about employee participation and industrial relations problems at BL. Needless to say, I jumped at the opportunity.

During my time in Germany with Seglow, I noticed how nervous he always seemed to be. As discreetly as I could, I mentioned this to him and expressed concern about how worried he often seemed to be. Peter explained that he fled to Britain from Austria just before WWII because of his Jewish nationality and he had an understandable mistrust of Germans.

On arrival at the Volkswagen plant, home of the Beetle family car, I was amazed how huge the factory was. It employed about 40,000 people all of whom were members of I G Metall, a union for the metal working trades. The factory was very modern. The gangways between production lines were very wide and clearly marked with yellow lines painted on the floor. Generally speaking it was very clean with no sign of arc and gas welding fumes and certainly no lead was being used to cover any design faults. Neither were there any air-powered tools, which create so much noise. Health and Safety notices were everywhere.

Workers were employed on a double-day shift system each of two hours. One of the production lines was nearly a mile long. During the other eight hours, mostly during the night, whole sections of production lines were lifted out by over-head cranes for maintenance work. Unheard of at Cowley!

Despite being a pre-war factory, Volkswagen was a well-constructed and well-maintained factory. It was also ten years ahead of Cowley so far as technology and employee rights were concerned. A good example about modern technology was on the door and chassis sections. At Cowley each car door was worked on separately. At Volkswagen, all four doors were clamped onto a huge round table with a crucifix. While an operator worked on one door, a robot worked on the other three. Once all four doors had been completed, the operator removed them to be replaced by the next set to be worked on. I also saw many examples similar to the door and chassis sections, which were technologically well in front of Cowley.

Despite the amount of modern technology, German car workers are no different from the British or any others in doing boring, uninspiring work on short time cycles, which the system compels if it is to be economic. I often wondered, whilst working under such circumstances myself, if consumers ever thought about the circumstances of workers who produce what they wish to buy. One advantage German car workers had, which we didn't, was that when they hung up their coats after clocking in at the beginning of each shift, they didn't also hang up their democratic and human rights at work like we used to, and still do in many companies.

No doubt WWII had caused much damage to the plant but it was quite clear from what I saw that Volkswagen had invested substantial sums of capital into the factory whereas, as I mentioned earlier, BL between 1968 and 1974 made a nett profit of £74 million and gave shareholders £70m in dividends with the remaining £4m invested in new plant and equipment.

As I was being guided round the plant I noticed a huge open space and asked why it was not being used for production or storage purposes. I was told the area was used by the management and union for reporting back to employees what the Board of Management was planning for the future. It was also used for the union representatives and management to report back on their discussions in the Supervisory Board. In view of the huge number of employees - up to 20,000 attending each meeting - it meant there had to be two meetings each time, some on a monthly basis.

At a meeting with a senior shop steward to exchange our different experiences, he was amazed to hear we had no such arrangement in the UK. Not surprisingly, he strongly supported the idea of unions having an 'influence' on management via the Supervisory Board. There was some criticism that the Board of Management made a decision contrary to what the Supervisory Board members had proposed but this was not developed in their comments.

Likewise, the Board of Management never saw this arrangement as challenging their right to manage. It was explained to me that the law of 'co-determination' in Germany precludes employers from determining unilaterally certain matters, which in Britain would be reserved as 'managerial functions'. The question needs to be asked, why if it works in Germany should it not work in Britain?

I am aware that some union members and militants in Britain will say we should never co-operate with management because that amounts to supporting the capitalist system. I take the view that we are very unlikely in the near future to end the days of working for capitalism (I only wish we could), so our main task should be to 'humanise' it and ensure through trade unions that employees have recognition and negotiating rights aimed at influencing management as the German workers are able to do on most matters important to them.

From my discussions with both management and union members during my visit I learnt a great deal about the importance of investment in new plant and equipment. It stood me in good stead for the next part of my visit to Germany, especially the lecture I was due to give that evening to a small group of German industrialists in West Berlin on employee participation.

Berlin

Our journey to Berlin was by car. On reaching the border between West and East Germany we had to throw our passports onto a covered conveyer belt, which crossed the 'no mans land' between West and East Germany. When they were eventually handed back, we were questioned for nearly thirty minutes by East German border security police as to why we wished to enter East Germany and why we had left West Germany. One of their main concerns seemed to be the fact that we were planning to stay in West Berlin. Eventually we were allowed to proceed on our journey when the police were satisfied with our answers and that we were not carrying anything, which could cause them concern. We arrived in West Berlin on a Friday. As we were not due to return to the UK until the following Monday this meant we had the whole weekend to spend as we wished.

We went sightseeing on our first day. One of our stops was on the West side of the Brandenburg Gate. We spent some time at the infamous Berlin Wall gazing into East Berlin and wondering what life must be like living there. On the Sunday we decided to visit East Berlin. This proved to be a totally different and frightening experience.

Having gained entry into East Berlin our first stop was on the side of the Brandenburg Gate looking west. We witnessed at first hand what authoritarian Communism was really like. A small car pulled up close to the Brandenburg Gate and a family got out to take a closer look. Within minutes armed police arrived and demanded the occupants remove everything from their car including their cases. Mum and Dad and the two children looked very frightened. Every case was emptied on to the ground and the contents searched. It all took about twenty minutes. Peter thought they were tourists from Hungary.

As Peter could speak German and we were close enough to hear what was being said, he gave me a running commentary about what the police were saying. When I suggested to Peter that we should complain about the way this family was being treated, he urged me not to say anything as the police might have thought that we knew the family and had planned to meet them there.

We left the scene as the police sent a very frightened family on their way and then we went to the famous square, Alexandra Platz. From there we caught a train and alighted at a station named Treptal Park. What we didn't realise at the time was that we were much nearer the Berlin Wall than was really safe. We had been told it was forbidden to take photographs of major road junctions, military establishments and factories. We soon found out why!

Peter Seglow said he wanted to find a factory, which had notices at the entrance reporting on the success of the workers in reaching their production targets. We soon found one - an electronics plant and Peter in no time got his camera out taking photographs of a huge sign about production targets and complimenting the workers for their efforts. Within minutes of Peter taking his pictures a door opened and several works police emerged with sub-machine guns and approached the entrance. At the same time, a vehicle came down the road and we were soon surrounded by armed men who never said a word. They were just very menacing.

Peter whispered to me, "Start admiring the buildings, etc. and they may realise we are not Americans." Despite the ugliness of most buildings we admired everything we saw in the hope it would work in our favour. As we slowly moved away, most of the armed police left, leaving only two who then stayed with us for the whole time we were in East Berlin. At no time was anything ever said to us by the police even when we returned to West Berlin. However, that was not the end of the matter.

On the Monday morning we were due to fly home from Templehof Airport, Berlin. At Passport Control we were singled out from other passengers, taken to a small room and questioned about why we had come to Berlin and where had we been during our stay. Our passports were removed for a time, no doubt to be photographed. No mention was made about East Berlin until we told them of our visit there. More questions were then asked about if we had taken any photographs and Peter had to admit he had taken some. We were then instructed to operate our cameras to prove they were really cameras. Peter's film of the factory was removed and confiscated. We were then allowed to board.

At Frankfurt we changed planes for Heathrow and had a further problem on arrival at Heathrow. Having passed through

Passport Control and made our way to Customs and Excise, we were both singled out again by a security officer and taken into a small room and questioned separately about where we had been and why? After about forty-five minutes we were allowed to proceed. My wife Beryl and our son Peter were waiting for me for over an hour and were very worried about what had happened to me, as they knew the plane had landed.

Ever since then a question has hung in my mind. What was the link between the East German and West German police in Berlin and a possible link between them and security police in London? I would love to know.

Part 2

Russian car and engineering plants

In November 1984 the TGWU General Secretary, Moss Evans decided to send me, as part of a three man team, to Russia on a seven day mission with the purpose of visiting car and engineering plants to study health and safety issues and report back. It was very strange that he should have asked me to go there as Beryl and I had been to Russia that very same year on holiday. We stayed in Moscow, Sochi and Leningrad (re-named St. Petersburg). I thought the contrast of going there as a tourist and then as part of an official union delegation would be interesting. And so it proved, for several reasons.

On our first visit my wife and I took nearly an hour going through Passport Control and Customs and Excise. On this second visit it was quite different because, as guests of the Government, we were allowed to pass through all the procedures very quickly with no questions asked. Nor were we searched for books and magazines they didn't want to enter the country. We left by a door not used by anyone other than special foreign visitors. Outside were several cars including a police car at the front and rear, waiting for us.

As we left the airport with the three Russian officials who had met us, the police put on their blue flashing lights and we travelled at high speed down the middle of the road towards central Moscow with all other vehicles being pushed to one side. Our hotel was named, 'Sputnik.' Not very original I thought. We were then shown to our rooms. Mine didn't impress me. It was very small, not very clean and had no hot water. A notice on the wall in the bathroom said, "Do not flush toilet paper down the lavatory pan, place it in the cardboard box beside the pan and it will be collected later." I discovered later that the paper was not regularly removed.

I decided to find where the leader of our delegation was and ask him to request from the hotel that I be given a better and cleaner room. Having obtained his room number, I went there to tell him of my situation. As he opened the door I was astonished to find he had a large hallway and a suite of rooms, which included a lounge and kitchen. It all looked very nice and clean. When I commented on this he said he had often been on union delegations to Moscow and every time delegation leaders always had higher standard rooms than the others. I was told I should make the most of it. It was an early lesson for me that there was a thriving class system within Russia. I saw further evidence of that during our seven days in Moscow and Minsk. Talk about double standards!

On our first morning we were taken to the famous Zil car factory, which we were told employed 50,000 people. Our three Russian minders stayed with us the whole time we were in the country. Zil cars are huge black cars, similar to the Rolls Royce and made exclusively for all senior government ministers. We were told Zil also made military vehicles but we were not allowed to see that part of the factory. The first part of the morning was taken up with a seminar on 'Health and Safety' at the plant. The seminar consisted of two senior managers presenting set speeches, all spoken in Russian. We were later given handouts in English of what they had said. The leader of our side, Grenville Hawley proposed a vote of thanks. When I asked if we were going to be able to make a contribution and ask questions, I was told, "No, you can read the handouts and maybe there will be time for discussion and questions another day." That opportunity never came!

At no time did we ever get involved in any questions or discussions about health and safety so I began to wonder why we were there. When I asked our leader for an explanation I was told that the TGWU were simply returning a 'Health and Safety' visit, which the Russians had made to Britain earlier in the year, and he did not see the need to get deeply involved in such matters as, 'given the state of their factories, it may embarrass our hosts'.

We spent the remainder of the morning touring the plant, which in many respects was very depressing because of the working conditions. Throughout, I have to say, I saw few signs of health and safety requirements. The shop floor was very uneven and there were many machines with moving parts but no safety guards. It was very dark in some areas as the lighting was nowhere near as strong at it should have been, bearing in mind the size of the production area. The condition of the factory reminded me of the Pressed Steel in the 1950s and 60s.

Whilst walking down one line, I asked one of our Russian minders who worked for Radio Moscow and was our interpreter throughout the seven days, to come with me as I wanted to ask one of the workers what life was like as a line operator. As I had been one for fourteen years, I knew what questions to ask. I nearly got to the production line when a senior manager called me back to the group and told the Russian off for agreeing to my request. I was told, "We have someone later on who you can speak to." Sure enough there was, but there were also two television cameras waiting for us and a line worker waiting to answer our questions. I thought at the time this may well be a set up for their evening news programme about English car workers visiting the factory. I declined the offer saying, "I would like to choose who I wish to speak to". A chance I never had. Our leader and the Russian management gave me some grim looks. I don't think either of them realised I wasn't looking at what I saw through rose tinted glasses. Having been a line operator for fourteen years, I knew what to look for in regard to health and safety issues.

Zil Car Works, Moscow, December 1984.
Attending a health and safety seminar

Lunch was my next shock. I was naïve enough to think we would eat in the workers' canteen. Not so! Fourteen of us were ushered into an oak-panelled dining room. A long table was heavily laden with red and black caviar in large quantities plus several bottles of vodka and apple juice. There was also a butler and the waiters were all dressed in black and white outfits. The dining room could have been mistaken for a top-class restaurant in London. The food was of a very high standard with cold meats and salad, huge steaks, plenty of vegetables and sweets followed by various cheeses.

No sooner had we started eating than our glasses were filled with vodka for a toast proposed by our host. Our host, having proposed the first one, I expected our leader to respond, and that would be end of toasting. However, each person was expected to propose a toast, fourteen in all. I tried not to drink too much before I had to propose a toast and talk about international friendship but I cannot remember what I said. We were informed it was a Russian custom that every drop should be drunk each time a toast was proposed. Somehow I managed to get away with not carrying out that custom. By the time we got to seven toasts, given the amount of vodka we had all drunk, with another seven to go, it was becoming impossible for people to speak coherently.

The lunch ended at 3.30 p.m. with our hosts saying, "Please don't be late for the formal dinner this evening at 7.30, which is part of our formal welcome to your delegation". The second meal that evening was a real struggle. We had spent the remainder of the afternoon at a small car component plant, which was equally in as bad a condition as the Zil factory so far as health and safety and conditions were concerned.

On our second day we were due to be collected from the hotel to go once again to the Zil factory. Due to a problem with the transport to collect us I agreed to go by taxi, which they laid on. I was accompanied by the Radio Moscow man acting as my interpreter. On our way across Moscow I asked him if he would be willing to put some questions to our driver, which he agreed to do. My first question was, "Do you own this taxi?"

He replied "No."

I then asked, "Would you like to own it?"

He replied, "Yes".

My next question was, "Would you like to own several taxis?"

Looking very excited he said, "Yes".

I then said, "Would you like to employ several people?"

Again the quick reply was, "Yes". It seemed to me from his replies that capitalism was alive and well even after sixty-seven years of Communism.

On arrival at the Zil factory and having toured other parts of the factory during the morning, we were taken to the works hospital. It had all the facilities you would expect we in this country would know as a Cottage Hospital. Four hundred and fifty beds, two fully equipped operating theatres, accident and emergency provision, dentistry, a maternity ward and a first aid centre for minor injuries.

Given the amount of works accidents, which we were told were very high, it came as no surprise they needed such a large hospital. In addition, we were informed that every employee and their relatives, including their children and grandparents, had a right to be treated and accepted if necessary into the hospital as a patient, provided there was a spare bed. Our discussions with the senior doctor centred on the issue of health and safety in the factory and the likely effect of dangerous fumes affecting workers' lungs, etc. Sadly all we had were comments such as, "It is a very safe place to work in, compared to some factories in the USSR". Like all the discussions we had while in Russia, no one seemed to think health and safety was a matter of major importance. They were more concerned about the need for high productivity.

At the end of our second day we boarded the night sleeper train from Moscow's main station for Minsk in Belorussia (now Belarus), with our three Russian minders at 11.00 in the evening to arrive at Minsk the following day at 8.00 a.m. We were due to spend two days visiting two engineering plants.

No sooner had we left Moscow than the train slowed to almost a crawl - about thirty-five miles per hour. We asked why and were told it was to help passengers to sleep. We later discovered it made no difference how fast or slow the train went because there were seven stations between Moscow and Minsk and at each station the loud public address system woke us up.

We arrived at Minsk at 8 a.m. to a freezing cold morning with a little snow - but much less than I expected at that time of the year.

With our three minders, plus some local minders, we set off in a small minibus after breakfast for our first visit to a factory 17 miles from Minsk. Travelling through the countryside and especially seeing so many miles of silver birch trees, famous in Belorussia, was a real treat.

One of the plants produced agricultural machinery including tractors and diesel engines. The other was producing dumper trucks for the iron ore industry quarries. Both factories were in a dreadful state.

The first factory we went to was like all the other factories we had been to in Moscow. I regret to say the machinery was all out of date and there was no sign of health and safety awareness. Walking down a final inspection line of diesel engines I saw an operator and mentioned that he looked too old to be doing such hard work. I asked one of our guides if the man was due to retire and had a shock when he replied, "No, he is only 42 years old". His rapid ageing came from the fact that diesel engines were being tested for efficiency and the building was constantly filed with diesel fumes, which he and other employees had to inhale. The leader of our delegation asked if it were possible for the men to be provided with protective clothing and a mask and was told, "It is not necessary".

The next factory we went to was by far and away the worst of those we had seen in Russia. Travelling through the factory to the main offices was a master class demonstrated by our driver, as he weaved his way through piles of rubbish and rusty machinery strewn across the road. There were no yellow lines to ensure the road was kept clear for traffic and pedestrians. The factory employed nearly 5,000 people with a good mixture of men and women all making the huge dumper trucks used in the iron ore industry.

We were struck how extremely cold it was and asked what the temperature was. They said it was -17°C outside and -11°C inside some parts of the factory. Workers had sacking tied round their arms, backs and legs, to try to keep warm. The lighting was very poor with many of the strip lights hanging on only one wire instead of being fixed properly to the roof. The shop floor was very greasy and, in some parts, dangerous to walk on.

We were not allowed to talk to any employees through our interpreter and spent the morning just wandering round the factory and like the employees, trying to keep warm. I was glad when lunchtime was mentioned and looked forward to some hot food.

Lunch was provided in the management dining room with the same generosity of food and drink we experienced in the Zil factory. I found myself sitting beside a member of the senior management who could speak a little English. During the meal he asked me what I thought about the factory. I do not regret being 'Jack Blunt' because of the reply he received. I said, "If this factory were in the UK, in the interests of my members I would have the place closed down on health and safety grounds". The leader of our delegation heard me and cautioned me to choose my words more carefully.

I then asked the manager why the factory was in such a terrible condition. I think his reply summed up for me why the Russian economy was in a mess. He replied, "I receive from the Central Committee in Belorussia on a yearly basis just enough funds to buy the raw materials I need to achieve my production targets. There is never enough left to carry out essential house keeping and to meet the needs of health and safety."

I then offered my solution. "What you need is sufficient capital to invest in new technology, which will enable you to decrease your unit costs. Furthermore, you need to reduce your labour force by a third and this would mean that, with the new technology, productivity would rise and the plant would be more competitive and efficient and much better for the employees to work in."

He replied, "The system will not allow that". His reply also meant that Russian factories were not the workers' paradise some had been led to believe. Maybe he was actually afraid of saying that the Government was frightened of modernising its major industries in case it caused mass unemployment followed by civil unrest.

It was then I concluded that the system did not deserve, and would not deserve, to survive beyond the end of the century. We all know it collapsed in 1991 for many obvious reasons.

Throughout all our visits to factories the Russians never once mentioned trade unions, shop stewards or health and safety representatives, which explained why we never met or had discussions with union officials.

Our last visit was to a kindergarten a few miles away and was run by the factory for the children of its employees. Compared to the two factories we had seen, it surprised me that every possible facility the children could wish for was provided. It was also obvious a great deal of money had been spent on their welfare. We were told that if any parents were ill or on holiday and could not care for their children they could stay in the kindergarten until their parents were able to take them home. Whilst we welcomed what facilities were being provided for relatives and their children, it seemed strange to us that a factory should be denied similar investment and better and safer conditions of work in the factory for its employees.

At the end of our second day we returned to Minsk after a farewell dinner given by our hosts and returned to Moscow on the night sleeper train arriving there at 8.00 the following morning.

Moscow

During breakfast we were told that plans had been made for us to have a conducted tour round Moscow and we would be picked up at 10.00 a.m. One of our minders who had not said a word throughout the whole visit arrived at the hotel with a minibus and in perfect English announced he was our tour guide for the day. We had been wondering all week why he didn't say a word and suspected he was a member of the KGB and had listened to all our conversations. We never asked, nor found out, why he kept silent.

Our first stop was at the Moscow Space Museum where we spent two hours seeing all the exhibits of space craft, including a mock-up of the rocket used by Yuri Gagarin in the 1960s to send him into space. We were also shown the capsule he used to return to earth.

We then went on a tour of the city and noticed wherever we went there were more buses and heavy goods vehicles than cars. Sitting beside me at the back of the minibus was the Moscow Radio man whom I had struck up a friendship with during the week. He was much more forthcoming to me about what he perceived were some of the failings of the communist system. A good example was when we were approaching Lubyanka Square. Our guide told us that if we looked down a small side road off the square we could just see the smallest shop in Moscow, which sold children's toys. My Russian friend whispered to me, "What he has not mentioned is the huge building we are just passing, which is the dreaded Lubyanka headquarters of the KGB where many political prisoners have been tortured and killed on Stalin's orders".

At the end of the tour we arrived in Red Square. We were told by our guide that we would be seeing the changing of the guard and visiting Lenin's tomb. The queue for the tomb looked very long and the prospects of standing for over an hour on a bitterly cold morning to get in was not a welcome prospect. However we were assured that it wouldn't be necessary and we were left to wonder why. I was able to film the changing of the guard, thanks to our 'minder' who waved his 'red card' to the police who then allowed me to leave the crowd and stand very close to the action.

As we were about to join the queue for the entrance to the tomb, we were told to follow our minder and we entered the queue about one hundred yards from the entrance much to the obvious anger of local people behind us. We later learned that it is quite normal for the queue to be held well back when Heads of State or important Ambassadors are making a visit and they go straight in. Others are allowed to enter the queue nearer the entrance according to their importance. We were about a hundred yards back, which indicated our level of importance.

Visitors enter the tomb in pairs and it fell to me to go down the steps to the entrance with our minder. As we entered the tomb I noticed there were guards standing in each corner who uttered 'shush' if anyone spoke.

All we could see of Lenin was his head and both fists. A bright light shone on his head and both fists but all the rest of his body was in darkness. As I left the tomb with the KGB man he said, "You do realise Mr. Buckle we Russians regard that place as our holy of holies".

I replied, "I would have thought you could have used a less spiritual term to describe that place".

Our final evening was spent in the Kremlin Palace of Congresses to see a wonderful performance of Georgian dancing.

As I boarded the plane to return home I had the same feeling as when my wife and I left Russia earlier that same year. I was glad to have been there, but also glad to being going home to what I believe with all its faults, is a more democratic and humane society. Anyone concerned about the well being of ordinary people in Russia must be concerned about the way things have turned out since 1991 when Communism (state capitalism as I have often described it) ended. It seems to me they have now gone from one extreme to another.

Conclusion

Readers may wonder why I have ended this small book about turbulent times at BL with memories of my visits to German and Russian car factories. I think if anyone believes that only the British car industry, and BL in particular, was a hotbed of militants they only have to look at the vast sums of capital invested in Volkswagen with very modern conditions, engineers everywhere on the shop floor compared to none in the Cowley factories. In addition, employees enjoy participation rights in Volkswagen that most British workers are denied which, if implemented, would have avoided so much turbulence.

In BL and Russian car factories, management were very production orientated and failed to give sufficient weight to the needs of their employees in terms of investment and decent conditions of employment or democratic rights through union rights. However, Russian workers were not allowed to protest or strike in the way workers at Cowley did.

This raises important reasons why workers should be allowed to join a union of their choice, which can negotiate freely and responsibly on their behalf about all matters affecting their jobs. They should not be expected to hang up their human rights with their coats when they clock on at the beginning of each shift.

As I have said previously and it bears repeating, I spent 24 years campaigning against right-wing management and militant shop stewards because the vast majority of our members deserved neither. It is no wonder to me that BL suffered so much turbulence, which a more caring management could have avoided and which would have denied extremists the opportunity to cause so much trouble for employees' job prospects and damage to a major car manufacturer.

What of the future for trade unions

Writing this small book set me wondering what the future of our trade unions will be. The harsh labour laws passed in the 1980s substantially increased the power of employers, as they were designed to do, over the rights of employees and reduced an effective role for unions to protect their members from authoritarian management. Prior to the late 1970s, Britain had a huge manufacturing base, which included coal mines, ship building and car factories all employing large numbers of employees - mostly trade unionist. I think I am right in saying that manufacturing amounted to about 65% of GDP in the early 1990s and has now shrunk to around 12% with a consequent reduction in trade union membership from nearly twelve million in the 1970s to six and half million in 2010.

Most of the existing union members are now in the public service sector, with the manufacturing industries having very few, due to unions finding it very difficult to recruit members or establish proper negotiating rights in many small firms. With major cuts coming in the public sector, membership even there is at risk. These are serious issues, which we must come to terms with and I want to suggest what lessons we should learn.

Most of the present harsh labour laws will remain, as neither of the major political parties wish to make any significant changes for fear of being seen as 'soft on unions'. I suggest the following policies are worth considering:

1. The TUC should become much more involved than it is at present with the International Labour Organisation (ILO), and use that organisation to press for changes in the current harsh labour laws.

2. I would modify the law in regard to strike ballots where the unions are expected to run an almost perfect system of contacting every member before the ballot is held. It is not generally known that the union must provide a list of the names and addresses of every employee receiving a ballot paper, which is an almost impossible task as people change their addresses even in the days prior to a ballot being held. Given that members also leave their job in the run up to a ballot, it is almost impossible to have a correct up-to-date list of who is entitled to vote. This opens the door to employers being able to rush off to court and obtain an injunction to stop the ballot or have a result declared invalid by a judge. No other organisation in the UK faces such serious scrutiny or is expected to be so accurate in conducting a ballot. That includes elections of MPs where some are elected on a minority of votes cast, unlike trade unions, which have to achieve 51% or more to succeed when proposing a strike. Trade unions are strictly regulated but not banks, which have the capacity to do far more damage to the economy than the unions ever contemplated, as we have all seen since the banking crisis in 2008.

3. Individual trade unions should start thinking internationally and begin linking up their activities with other national unions where they have common interests with major international companies that operate over several national borders. A good example of that would be the automotive industry both in Europe and the Far East.

4. Trade unions should be campaigning for the right of employees to join a union at their place of work and the right to recognition for bargaining purposes plus genuine employee participation agreements.

Long ago, the TUC called for a charter of employee rights to protect all people at work and not just trade unionists. They suggested the following:

i   A right to work in a safe and healthy environment in the certain knowledge that standards will be enforced by law.

ii   Stronger rights to safeguard people against unfair dismissal or unfair redundancy.

iii   The right to fair wages and conditions, including stronger powers to set minimum standards on hours of work and holidays.

iv   Rights to time off work without loss of pay for education and training.

v   Effective laws to prevent discrimination in employment on grounds of race and sex.

The TUC suggest that the above rights should apply to all workers, regardless of the size of their company or public service. I hope it's not wishful thinking on my part that one day a Charter of Rights is established in law for all workers, which will bring democracy to the work place. It would certainly reduce the opportunity for authoritarian management and may even be the beginning of their having a more caring attitude towards their employees.

Books and reports about the motor industry

Compiled by David Buckle. April 2010

This is a selection of books and reports, which I hope will prove useful to those who are interested in finding out more about the subject and why the British Car Industry self-destructed in the 1980s and 90s.

Andrews and Brunner. *Life of Lord Nuffield.* Oxford. 1955.

G Turner. *The Car Makers.* London. Eyre and Spottiswoode. 1963.

H A Turner, G Clack and G Roberts. *Labour Relations in the Motor Industry,* London. Allen and Unwin. 1967.

G Turner. *The Leyland Papers.* Eyre and Spotteswoode. 1971.

Rys. *The British Motor Industry.* (An economic survey) London. Butterworth. 1972.

H Beynon. *Working for Ford.* London. Penguin. 1973.

E Wigham. *The Power to Manage.* London. MacMillan. 1973.

Sir Don Ryder. *British Leyland: The Next Decade.* Her Majesty's Stationary Office. 1973.

K Richardson. *The British Motor Car Industry. A social and economic history.* London. MacMillan. 1977.

M Edwardes. *Back from the Brink.* Collins. London. 1983.

R C Whiting. *The Views From Cowley. The Impact of Industrialisation upon Oxford, 1918 - 1939.* Oxford Historical Society. 1983.

W Streeck. *Industrial Relations in West Germany.* Heinemann. London. 1984.

P Williams and G Winch. *Innovation and management control. Labour Relations at BL Cars.* Cambridge University Press. 1985.

D Marsden, T Morris, P Williams, S Wood. *Social Science.* Paperback. Tavistock Publications. London. 1985.

J Jones. *Union Man (A union view).* London. Collins. 1986.

K Williams, J Williams and C Haslam. *The Breakdown of Rover, A Case Study in the Failure of Business Strategy and Industrial Policy.* Berk Publishers. 1987.

P Wickens. London. *The Road to Nissan.* 1988.

M Adeney. *The Motor Makers. The Turbulent History of Britain's Car Industry.* Collins. London. 1988.

D J Buckle and J Greenhough. *Hostilities Only. Autobiography.* Robert Dugdale. Oxford. 1999.

Car Company takeovers

Compiled by David Buckle MBE JP

1952   Austin-Morris merges into British Motor Corporation.

1953   BMC takes over Fisher and Ludlow.

1961   Jaguar takes over Daimler. Leyland takes over Standard Triumph.

1964   Chrysler buys a share of Rootes Group.

1966   Pressed Steel Company merges with Fisher and Ludlow and becomes part of BMC.

1966   BMC and Jaguar merge as British Motor Holdings.

1967   Chrysler takes over Rootes Group. In the same year the Rootes Group announce withdrawal of all car body production from the Pressed Steel, Cowley because of its merger with BMC. This deprives the Pressed Steel of 47% of car body production.

1968   Leyland and BMC merge to form BLMC.

1980   BL and Honda buy 20% of each other's shares. No formal link.

1986   BL renamed Rover Group. The car division is named Austin Rover Cars Ltd. and is privately owned.

1988   BAe buys the Rover Group from the Government saying they only want to own it for five years.

1994   April. BMW take over the Rover Group from BAe.

Union/management ballot results in BL
1977 – 1980
Compiled by David Buckle.

OCTOBER 1977

On bargaining reform.

BL run, manual employees only.

Yes   59,029   65.34%

No   31,304   34.65%

       90,333   Total eligible to vote   103,605

APRIL 1978

On Company-wide incentive scheme.

Unions run.

Yes   21,759   32,02%

No   46,106   67,86%

       67,865   Total eligible to vote   97,000

DECEMBER 1978

On Parity Pay for all Manual employees.

BL run.

Yes   48,702   65.72%

No   25,403   34.27%

       74,105   Total, eligible to vote   95,000

OCTOBER 1979

On Edwardes' recovery plan.

BL run.

Blue and White collar employees

Yes	106,062	87.27%		
No	15,541	12.78%		
	121,603	Total eligible to vote	166,603

FEBRUARY 1980 *

1979/80 TU rejection of pay offer.

Unions run.

Manual employees only.

Yes	41,422	59.13%		
No	28,623	40.86%		
	70,045	Total eligible to vote	85,155

*This ballot was organised by the Confederation of Ship Builders and Engineering Unions (CONFED) on behalf of BL Unions.

As described in an earlier chapter, despite unions winning a majority against the Company-Wide Incentive Scheme and the 1980 pay offer, BL, having agreed to the ballots, refused to accept the results and imposed their schemes and pay offer in April 1980. The imposition of this destroyed all trust in ballots as a means of resolving industrial relation problems in BL.